INSIDE SPINAL TAP

INSIDE
SPINAL TAP

PETER OCCHIOGROSSO

ABACUS

An Abacus *Book*

First published in the USA in 1985 by Arbor House Publishing Company
First published in this revised edition in Great Britain in 1992 by Abacus

Copyright © 1985, 1992 by Peter Occhiogrosso

All photos not otherwise credited are reproduced
by courtesy of Embassy Pictures.

The moral right of the author has been asserted.

A CIP catalogue record for this book
is available from the British Library.

ISBN 0 349 10459 X

Printed and bound in Great Britain by
BPCC Hazells Ltd

Abacus
A Division of
Little, Brown and Company (UK) Limited
165 Great Dover Street
London SE1 4YA

**To my mother,
for not telling me to turn
the damn thing down
any more than she had to**

CONTENTS

Acknowledgments ix

Author's Preface xiii

Spinal Tap:
The (Somewhat) Definitive
    Bio 1

Spinal Tap Redivivus 4

Tapping an American Vein:
    A Band for Our (Hard)
    Times 12

They Remember Spinal Tap
Jeanine Pettibone-St.
Hubbins 16
Mike Pym 17

They Died Before They Got
Old:
    A Concise Guide to
    Spinal Tap's
    Drummers 18

Tap Alive:
    Spinal Tap on 20
    "Saturday Night Live"

"Christmas with the
    Devil" 23

Afterthought: Tufnel on Tap
    on SNL 24

A Note of Warning 25

Spinal Tap Meets the
    Press 28

Tap on Wheels 32

The World of Spinal Tap 38

Girls Who Got to Meet the
    Boys 39

My Beautiful Experience
    with Spinal Tap 44

The ABC's of Spinal Tap:
    A Luv Poem 45

Personnel Files
    Nigel Tufnel 46
    David St. Hubbins 51
    Derek Smalls 57

The Beat Goes On 63

Spinal Rap 65
    David and Derek Come
    Clean

Guitar Stars
    David St. Hubbins 68
    Nigel Tufnel 73

Their Top Ten
    David St. Hubbins 78
    Derek Smalls 78
    Nigel Tufnel 80

Wise Up! 81

Star Flap
    David St. Hubbins 85

A Day to Forget
Nigel Tufnel 88

Roots
    Derek Smalls 89

The Aesthetics of Spinal
    Tap: A Critical
    Essay 91

Joe on Tap 94

The Joe Franklin Show:
    Tap on Joe 95

Final Tap
    Live in Seattle: A
    Concert Memoir 99

Looking Back
    David and Nigel
    Remember
    Seattle 104

Toward a Critical
    Tapography 106

Addendum 111

ACKNOWLEDGMENTS

First of all, of course, I want to thank the entity that is Spinal Tap merely for being, and thus for providing the raw material out of which this book was lovingly hewn. Long may they rock.

In addition, I am grateful to Bobbi Cowan for having arranged my initial contacts with the members of Tap, and to Randi Wershba and Nancy Seltzer for their continuing assistance in this matter. Special thanks to Rhonda Markowitz of Polymer Records, an unselfish rocker in the all-too-thankless arena of record publicity, for her help and enthusiasm throughout the project—and mainly for all those free T-shirts.

Karen Murphy, producer of the rockumentary film *This Is Spinal Tap*, was generous and extremely helpful in selecting photo material from the movie and contributing several wonderful photos of her own.

Others who provided invaluable assistance include Walter Calmette and Lee Rosenbaum for oiling the machinery at Embassy Pictures; Terri Kilroy for her gracious help in making the Embassy photo files available; Audrey Dickman, Holly Browde, and Joe Franklin for their kind assistance in clearing portions of this book for publication; my friend Paul Slansky for helping to provide an inside track.

An extra-special thanks to Margery Dignan for her careful reading and knowledgeable improvements of the text, and for her endless encouragement.

I offer a special paragraph of thanks to the many photographers, known and unknown, whose pictures tell the story—especially to Steve Meltzer for his wonderful work in Seattle, and to Laurie Paladino and Harry Shearer.

And for research assistance above and beyond the call of heavy duty, Taphead *extraordinaire* Michael McKean. Finally, I would like to thank my agent, Susan Breitner, for being visionary enough to agree that there *was* a book in all this, even though she'd never heard "Hell Hole" or "Big Bottom"—and my editor at Arbor House, Helen Eisenbach, for initiating the project, even though she *had* heard them.

Q: Do you think you'll always be famous?

DAVID ST. HUBBINS: No, but *we'll* always remember us.

I first met the boys who formed the "core" of Spinal Tap in London in 1975. It was a troubled time for the band, as it was for the whirligig world of rock 'n' roll in general. Morris Albert's classic "Feelings" nuzzled the likes of Glen Campbell, John Denver, and the Captain and Tennille in the upper reaches of the Billboard Hot 100. Silver Convention, the Bee Gees, and K.C. and the Sunshine Band bumped booties on disco turntables around America. The Eagles and the Doobies represented the "best" of stateside rock (for *rock* had indeed supplanted *rock 'n' roll* as the critic's term of choice). Van McCoy "hustled" his way to Number One for a week, and even little Janis Ian had a Top Ten hit. The postglam world of Britain sent us Elton John and Bowie, though they were more than offset by the Sweet, Bad Company, Paul McCartney and Wings, and the Bay City Rollers. And then there was Spinal Tap.

In what appears in retrospect to have been one of the great minor-key introductions of my journalistic career, I strolled unsuspecting one day into an East Squatney pub called the Grub & Hangdog only to find David St. Hubbins and Nigel Tufnel—inseparable as ever—engaged in a snarling argument over the check. I stood at the door for a long moment, sunset rays streaming over my shoulder, and just took in the sight. Then I approached.

David and Nigel, Nigel and David, two names intertwined in rock history as closely as John and Paul, Mick and Keith, Phil and Don, Barry, Robin, and . . . well, David and Nigel. That year of '75 they had just returned from a tour of the Far East and released their second live album (after *Silent but Deadly*), the three-LP set *Jap Habit*, and had filed suit against their record label, Megaphone, for withholding royalties. (Megaphone, in its own rather petty, tit-for-tat style, threatened to countersue the band for "lack of talent." The whole matter was resolved out of court when the band agreed to cease recording for the Megaphone ingrates and generally to "stay the fuck out of the studio," as their solicitor told *Rolling Stone*.)

It was therefore with an equal mixture of tingling anticipation and ill-concealed awe that I edged over to the two figures sequestered at a prime corner table and haltingly introduced myself as the American journalist who had long championed their cause (for so I saw the shame of their treatment, or lack thereof, at the hands of my colleagues). Imagine my surprise and immense gratification when they both looked up, regarding me somewhat dubiously at first but not without a certain modicum of inchoate curiosity. As the clouds of obfuscation gently dissipated from before their brows—as if the very sun at my back had served to part the mists of their pettifogging preoccupation—nascent smiles formed along the coastlines of first David's and then Nigel's still-young lips.

Momentarily loosening his hold on Nigel's throat, David offered me a hand in greeting. And though that same hand (mine, not his) had shaken with the likes of Lennon, Bowie, and Brown, I considered it a distinct *experience* at last to come to grips, as it were, with one of the most elusive spirit/beings of the rock 'n' roll cosmos. Then Nigel, too, warily lay down the Sheffield carving knife he held tightly in his fist and likewise extended a hand—fingers shaped curiously in the configuration of an E^7 chord, open tuning—and shook lustily.

For a while all was small talk and frippery as I jockeyed for position in classic journalist-meets-rock-stars-whom-he-sees-as-potential-big-bucks-feature-interview-material-but-whom-he'd-also-like-to-be-able-to-call-his-friends-without-sucking-up-too-much fashion. What had Japan really been like? What had Japanese *girls* really been like? Wasn't Megaphone a suck-ass company to begin with? Whose idea was it to include two pounds of gimmick packaging with the triple-live *Jap Habit*? What was the true story behind Ross MacLochness's departure from the band and, by turns, did they feel that Viv Savage would prove out on keyboards? Why did their drummers keep dying on them? And, many Guinnesses later, who would finally pick up the check?

All these questions and more were tossed about—some were caught, some dropped dismally onto the sawdust of the Grub & Hangdog's mangy floor, and some simply faded into the stale air to be washed down with stale stout and the odd packet of crisps. Squatney dusk became Squatney gloaming became Squatney night.

And we never did seem to get around to the really big questions —the ones that burn in your gut at night when you try in vain to make some sense out of the world and the lumps in your pillow, when the premise of sleep ever coming is like a long, long guitar solo that goes on for chorus after ,agonized chorus without ever really finding its way back to the key in which it began, which the guitarist has long since forgotten and which no amount of string-bending or frantic jump-kicks over micro-phone stands will jar his memory into retrieving, and for which, ultimately, the rest of the band wait and wait, like faithful Penelopes at first and then like

characters in some Beckett play and finally—well, but I'm digres-sing here. What I *do* know for certain is that somewhere amid all the Guinness and darts and even a hasty meal of bangers and mash (I can't say as I know the Yank equivalent of that one), there was born in me a longing, a yearning to know more, that has become a lifelong fascination—although some "friends" of mine presume to refer to it as "the fas-cination of repulsion," like when the hyperacned face of some wretched teenager grabs and holds our attention despite our better instincts to look away, look away. This paragraph is too long.

So began my interest in Spinal Tap, the *people*. Later on, when I met bassist *extraordinaire* Derek Smalls (the name, the verbal pack-aging, as is so often the case, belies the true nature of what is contained within!), then the points of my personal compass— the triangulation that would steer my destiny with laserlike clarity over the next decade of otherwise unfocused, impover-ished existence—were complete. These three prongs of my trident, so to speak, which I would hurl at an unfriendly gladiatorial foe —god, how I hate the inadequacy of these metaphors. Suffice it to say that coming to the band as they had come to each other— first Nigel and David and then Derek—I knew what I had to do from then on.

And I did it.

What follows now is simply the cream, the wheat (the Cream of Wheat?), the molten metal (yes!) freed from the dross and slag of the many articles, stories, inter-views, news items, transcripts of appearances (live and "on the air"), fan offerings of apprecia-tion, and even letters of warning,

which I have collected and collated over the years since our fateful meeting in that humble-yet-exquisite Squatney public house. (The thought of erecting a plaque of sorts there has crossed and crisscrossed my mind more than once. Unfortunately, the pub has long since been torn down.)

I bequeath this collection to you, the faithful public, in the same spirit of generous indulgence with which the Men of Tap gave so graciously of themselves in the many interviews and exchanges here gathered in print for the first time ever. I am tempted to quote to you the words of the writer Sean O'Faolain to readers of Joyce's *Portrait of the Artist as a Young Man*: "Enter these enchanted woods, ye who dare...." Much is to be learned from these records, even more to be passed over quickly. Yet it is truly all of a piece, a history that says a lot about the world we live in, the way we are and the way we were, among other things.

I make no pretense of judging Spinal Tap on the merits of their various *oeuvres*. That is for smaller, more critical minds than mine (see R. Seltzer, p. 91). For one thing, I find myself quite in-capable of the kind of steel-edged objectivity required to genuinely appraise so elusive an art as that of rock 'n' roll music, or such de-ceptively gossamer poesy as the rock lyric. To me, Spinal Tap are larger than Rock 'n' Roll Life; they exist outside the petty course of day-to-day musical excellence. In a word, they simply *are*. It is in that sense that I may truly say then—as distinct from the well-known film that hardly, *hardly* did them justice as musical art-ists *or* as People—*THIS Is Spinal Tap*!

—**Peter Occhiogrosso**
Somewhere in America, 1985

Spinal Tap

The (Somewhat) Definitive Bio

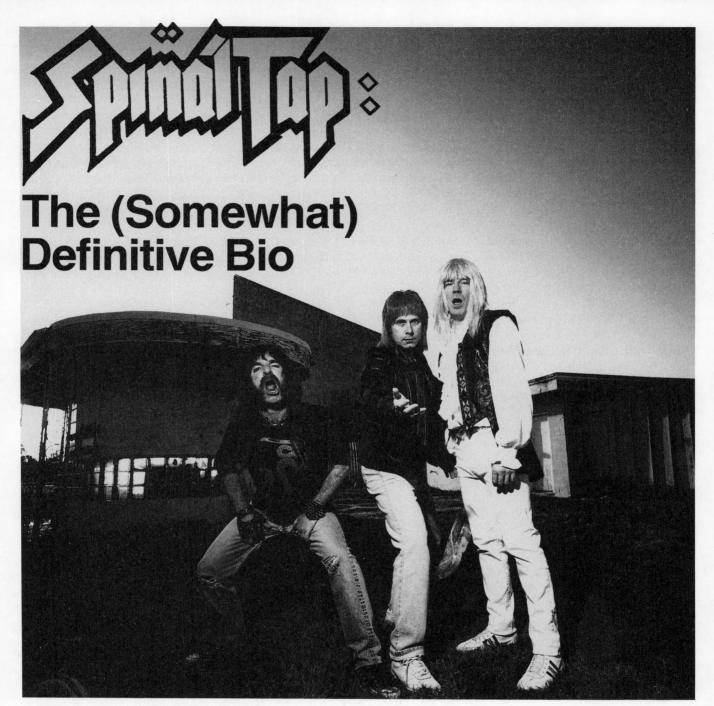

Rock's living palimpsest. (Photo by Sylvia Otte.)

The following is culled from several band biographies of Spinal Tap, issued variously by Megaphone, Polymer, and Dead Faith/MCA Records. Some of this information has been known to long-time Tap aficionados, handed down over the years from fan to fan in the great oral tradition of the Buddhist Patriarchs and the Hindu Brahmans. But although an abridged version of the earlier material did appear in the ever-popular *Rocklopedia Brittanicus* (p. 743), and in the American edition of this book, the full extent of Tap's checkered history has never before been published. It is as definitive as one can hope for a band whose history is filled with so many mysterious inconsistencies and gaping lacunae.

◆

NIGEL TUFNEL and DAVID ST. HUBBINS grew up in the same city block in London's Squatney District, where David played guitar in a skiffle band, the CREATURES, while Nigel did the same for the LOVELY LADS. The two began jamming together outside tube stations, and eventually formed their first legitimate band, the ORIGINALS, later changed to the NEW ORIGINALS when the East End ORIGINALS (now the REGULARS) threatened suit.

The New Originals collapsed in 1964 without record company support, but David and Nigel were hired by the legendary JOHNNY GOODSHOW REVUE and played the Seaside Circuit, gigging after hours at local pubs. It was in a Southampton tavern, the Bucket (now the Bucket and Pail), that they met and jammed with JOHN "STUMPY" PEPYS, then drummer for the LESLIE CHESWICK SOUL EXPLOSION (now LES and MARY CHESWICK).

When the weather turned cold, the three hooked up with bassist RONNIE PUDDING from the CHEAP DATES (now CHEAPDATE) and began working in London as the THAMESMEN. They released their debut single on Abbey, "GIMME SOME MONEY" b/w "CUPS AND CAKES," in late spring, 1965. It did not hit the charts immediately.

Meanwhile, the band played extensively in the Benelux nations, particularly Amsterdam's Long-Hair Club, where they met sixteen-year-old keyboard prodigy JAN VAN DER KVELK, who did musical charts for the band and used his Dutch music-biz connections to get them work. Leaving Amsterdam and Van Der Kvelk behind, the band returned to Britain as the DUTCHMEN and found "Gimme Some Money" climbing the charts. The band quickly changed their name *back* to the Thamesmen but the single had peaked and vanished from sight.

During the next eighteen months the group performed under the following names: RAVE BREAKERS, HELLCATS, FLAMIN' DAEMONS, SHINERS, MONDOS, the DOPPEL GANG, the PEOPLES, LOOSE LIPS, WAFFLES, HOT WAFFLES, SILVER SERVICE, the MUD BELOW, and the TUFNEL-ST. HUBBINS GROUP.

Its personnel included: NICK WAX, TONY BRIXTON, DICKY LAINE, and DENNY UPHAM (keyboards); JIMMY ADAMS, GEOFF CLOVINGTON (horns); JULIE SCRUBBS-MARTIN, LHASA APSO (backing vocals); and, briefly, LITTLE DANNY SCHINDLER (vocals, harmonica), later with the SHVEGMAN-HAYMAN-KVELKMAN BLUES BAND FEATURING LITTLE DANNY SCHINDLER, now powerful record executive LITTLE DANIEL SCHINDLER. (Shvegman, Hayman and Kvelkman later signed with CPR Records as TALMUD.)

Tufnel, St. Hubbins, Pudding, Upham and Stumpy played their first gig as SPINAL TAP at the Music Membrane in December, 1966. Tap's debut single, released in July, 1967, on Megaphone, was "(LISTEN TO THE) FLOWER PEOPLE" b/w "RAINY DAY SUN." The A-side was penned by Ronnie Pudding, who left the band when "Flower People" became a hit to form PUDDING PEOPLE. Subsequent Pudding product on Megaphone (single, "I Am the Music," and album, *I Am More Music*) went nowhere. He was replaced on bass by DEREK SMALLS, formerly with England's pioneer all-white Jamaican showband, SKAFACE. When Skaface broke up following the 1965 Boxing Day riots, Smalls "gave up rock 'n' roll" and enrolled in the London School of Design as a design major. He reemerged with MILAGE for their only album, *Milage I*, then gigged semi-extensively around London 'til Spinal Tap beckoned. With a hit single under their belts, the band recorded their first album, *Spinal Tap* (released in the States as *Spinal Tap Sings "(Listen to the) Flower People" and Other Favorites*). The LP was produced by GLYN HAMPTON-CROSS who has guided much of Tap's subsequent output.

The album went gold, but on the follow-up LP, *We Are All Flower People*, sales, when they occurred, were disappointing. The band panicked, fired keyboardist Upham, and toured as a four-piece band, supporting the then-hot MATCHSTICK MEN. Under the headliners' tutelage they developed the heavier acid based, twin guitar attack which earmarks Spinal Tap product to this day.

Spinal Tap made their biggest splash at the now-legendary Electric Zoo concerts in Wimpton, culminating in the then-legendary two-hour St. Hubbins/Tufnel guitar solo on "Short and Easy." The live recordings of the Zoo shows yielded the third Tap album, *Silent But Deadly*, which established them as a top draw.

The tragic death of "Stumpy" Pepys in a bizarre gardening accident left the band stunned, saddened and holding auditions for a new drummer. They settled on ERIC "STUMPY JOE" CHILDS (from WOOL CAVE) and recorded such LPs as: *Brainhammer, Blood to Let, Nerve Damage, Intravenus de Milo*, and the "Concept" album *The Sun Never Sweats*. For *Sweats* they hired keyboard player ROSS MACLOCHNESS (ex-KILT KIDS) and brought in session drummer PETER "JAMES" BOND to replace Stumpy Joe, whose death was even more macabre than his predecessor's.

In 1975, Spinal Tap toured the Far East and released their second live set, *Jap Habit*—three discs and two pounds of gimmick packaging. Ross MacLochness left to do missionary work in Namibia, later releasing one solo LP, *Doesn't Anybody Here Speak English?* He was replaced by VIV SAVAGE (of AFTERTASTE), for the poor-selling *Bent for the Rent*. The band sued Megaphone for withholding royalties. The label threatened a precedent-setting countersuit charging "lack of talent." By way of settlement the band agreed to make no further records for Megaphone and, in the words of their solicitor, to "stay the fuck out of the studio."

The group retreated to Nigel's castle in Scotland to ponder their future and pursue solo projects. Only one of these saw the light of day, *Nigel Tufnel's Clam Caravan*. Derek Smalls' projected solo album, *It's a Smalls World*, exists only as an eight-track "super demo."

In the late spring of 1977, "Nice 'n' Stinky," a live cut from the two-year-old *Jap Habit*, became a huge surprise hit in America. Capitalizing on this momentum, Spinal Tap regrouped with drummer MICK SHRIMPTON (once drummer with the Eurovision Song Contest house band), replacing Peter "James" Bond who had spontaneously combusted on stage during the "Isle of Lucy" Jazz Festival. They also released a new album on Polymer Records, *Shark Sandwich*, which yielded some "airplay hits" and reestablished TAP as a contender.

To launch its fourteenth album, *Smell the Glove*, Spinal Tap returned to America—after a six-year absence—for a soon-to-be-legendary cross-country tour. That tour was, of course, the subject of the much-ballyhooed and now disputed "rockumentary" *This Is Spinal Tap*, by the American film- and commercial-maker MARTIN DiBERGI. Released in 1984, the film follows the band across America, through a change of managers and a temporary parting of the ways, and climaxes with the band's dramatic reunion for a last-minute tour of Japan, with new drummer JOE "MAMA" BESSER replacing the ill-fated Mick Shrimpton, who had mysteriously exploded onstage.

When the Japanese tour self-destructed shortly after it began in the fall of 1982, Tap went into yet another hiatus, only to reemerge in the States for a whirlwind year of promotional appearances in 1984 after the movie brought them briefly back into the public consciousness. When no major record or performance offers were forthcoming, however, the members went their separate ways until they were once again reunited at the funeral of their erstwhile manager, IAN FAITH, eight years later. Replacing drummer Besser, who had disappeared under mysterious circumstances, with Mick Shrimpton's younger (by 20 minutes) twin brother RICHARD ("RIC") SHRIMPTON, the band released their first new album in ten years, *Break Like the Wind*. Sadly, long-time keyboardist Viv Savage had also perished in a freak natural-gas explosion while visiting the elder Shrimpton's gravesite. He was deemed irreplaceable. Instead, several famous guest artists and producers were brought in to add new lustre to Tap's line-up.

And the rest, as they say, is hysteria.

Spinal Tap Redivivus

by Neil Witherspoon

"Good morning, New Orleans!" (Photo by Sylvia Otte.)

David St. Hubbins, gold tresses streaming in the bright lights, looks almost elfin in a red night-shirt that comes to mid-thigh, showing a devilish amount of leg. Derek Smalls, with his trademark muttonchop mous-tache and sporting a green and gold silk dressing-gown with black cuffs and fringes, could pass for a Middle-Eastern pasha (well, a cute, hairy one, any-way). And the usually gruff Nigel Tufnel looks positively cuddly in rumpled blue and white striped cotton pajamas.

Breakfast with Spinal Tap in their lavish hotel suite, sur-rounded by fawning publicists? A sleepwear fashion shoot for

Esquire? Not bloody likely, mate. No, never a band to do things the easy way, Tap are in fact playing their latest gig, an 11:00 A.M. "breakfast" show for a hall full of music industry conventioneers in New Orleans, who are screaming and clapping like a bunch of hyper-hormoned teenagers.

The night before, Tap arrived for their 1:00 A.M. soundcheck only to learn that certain record company honchos had deftly usurped Tap's relatively early spot for their own bands, forcing David, Nigel, and Derek to wait until 4:00 A.M. to begin a two-hour soundcheck. The boys took it philosophically, but they

barely had time to catch a few winks before hitting the stage. Forget about eating breakfast or getting *dressed*! Some rock 'n' roll bands have been accused of practically playing in their sleep, but for these more-than-veteran British rockers, doing it in their pajamas is the next best thing.

Besides, the symbolism is per-fect. Hardly loath to jump on a time-tested bandwagon, Tap seems to have discovered—some years after a recent US president coined the slogan—that it's Morning in America. While some of the locals might have reason to doubt the truth of that in today's depressed economic climate, Spinal Tap can smell

"No time to rest, no time to shower . . ." (Photo by Sylvia Otte.)

of a diabetic. A little too much insulin here, not enough sucrose there, suddenly a big, dizzying plunge and then, ahhhh—a quick injection of sophisticated production values on their new CD results in just the right mix of primal, rough-hewn songs and state-of-the-art sound quality to produce a stable heartbeat.

For anyone who might have spent the last two decades in an ashram in Rishikesh, Spinal Tap's early history is easily recapped; with the usual flurry of false starts and name changes; it may even seem relatively normal. But soon, as the DiBergi film memorably recounts, things began to go ever so slightly awry. For openers, Tap's drummers started dying off mysteriously, the first in what the band describes as a "bizarre gardening accident," another bursting into flames in a rare case of spontaneous combustion, yet another in an onstage explosion. Then, in the 1982 American tour documented in the film, the band got lost on their way to the stage at a concert in Cleveland. A crucial article of stage scenery for an epic production number came out looking like a piece of doll house furniture. A luckless Derek was trapped inside one of the giant plastic pods used during the band's rendition of "Rock and Roll Creation," and, freed at last, was nearly decapitated when he tried to get back in. Finally the tour began to unravel, along with Tap's manager Ian Faith, a pale and bloated-looking chap who seemed to fend off an incipient nervous breakdown only by keeping a firm grip on his beloved cricket bat. Faith clashed openly with St. Hubbins's New Age ice-queen girlfriend Jeanine Petti-bone and later quit, leaving

the coffee—and it ain't decaf. After coming to the general public's attention in 1984 through the revealing but, as the band now insists, cruelly flawed Marty DiBergi "rockumentary" *This Is Spinal Tap*, and disbanding soon afterwards, Spinal Tap is back banging louder than ever on fortune's door. Their first new album in eight years, *Break Like the Wind*, has just been released on their very own MCA specialty label, Dead Faith, to eagerly awaited reviews. Their world tour, which begins in May, will culminate in a gig at London's legendary Royal Albert Hall that will be filmed and spun off into a fall TV special. It's beginning to look as though the American public is

once again resonating in a big way with the blue-collar bonhomie of Spinal Tap—their unique ability to give voice to the existential urgencies of life that we all feel, in songs like "Big Bottom," "Heavy Duty," and "Hell Hole," but to do it with a smile. The final canonization will take place later this month when that high priest of good ol' Yankee corner-cutting, everyman extraordinaire Bart Simpson, attends a Spinal Tap concert in a new episode of *The Simpsons*.

Still, the chart of Tap's rise and fall and rise and fall and rise would probably look less like the Dow Jones average and more like the blood sugar count

Jeanine to manage the band with little more than blonde ambition and home-made astrological charts.

The movie appeared to end on a high note, with the band invited to tour Japan, but that tour ended in disaster shortly after it began. Tap took a brief curtain call following the release of the DiBergi film in '84, making the odd promotional appearance, giving print interviews, and showing up on such American TV institutions as *Saturday Night Live* and the *Joe Franklin Show*, but they soon faded into what promised to be an early retirement. So when word of their reunion after an eight-year hiatus reached me, I was eager to hear firsthand what had happened in Japan and what the band had been doing since. And New Orleans sounded like as good a place as any to meet up with them because, like these perennial musical legends, the city has a glorious heritage that seems ever so frayed about the edges. On historic Bourbon Street, for instance, the jazz clubs are outnumbered ten to one by topless bars and souvenir T-shirt emporia. And hung-over executives from the radio merchandising and Jiffy-Lube conventions wander the streets of the French Quarter, staggering into indignant tourists wearing "I Survived Mardi Gras" paraphernalia even as the sidewalks are rinsed with disinfectant.

Tap, of course, are safely insulated from all this in their MCA limo as we drive around looking for likely photo sites. Slowly—the band is a bit groggy themselves after that morning gig and a suspiciously long lunch break—the story of the Japan fiasco unfolds. After playing their first show in a city whose name none of them can recall, Tap was so jet-lagged from the long flight over that they slept for 18 hours straight, effectively missing the next concert and the soundcheck for the one after *that*. "They take everything so personally," says Derek, scratching a stubbled chin. "The next day this tiny little man with a bullet-head is standing in our hotel room saying, 'You have shamed a respected rock 'n' roll promoter and his entire nation.' And we're thinking, What kind of nation has *respected* rock 'n' roll promoters?"

"You sleep through a couple of scheduled concerts and suddenly you're a traitor to the Emperor," says David with a toss of the famous St. Hubbins locks. "The real problem was that we just weren't the flavor of the month anymore. By the time we got to Japan the single had already peaked anyway." The tour summarily canceled, they made their separate ways back home.

And now in New Orleans, home of Jelly Roll Morton, Fats Domino, and the world's most entertaining funerals, they reflect on the irony behind their reunion. It seems that the three of them met up at the wake of their erstwhile manager, whom Derek refers to blithely as "the late ingrate Ian Faith." David ruefully alleges the cause of death was "an overdose of royalties," and says the band was hoping they might collect some of the funds still owed them from Faith's estate. They didn't get their money, but they discovered something even better.

"It was really one of the happiest occasions I can remember in the last half-century," Nigel recalls fondly as he eyes a passing gaggle of Spring Break college girls in tight white shorts. "People laughing and dancing around, running by the coffin and tweaking his nose."

"Taking the coins off his eyes," Derek adds, "and putting I.O.U.s there. I'd never seen that." Even the fact that Tap got stuck with the $11,000 tab for the buffet at the wake didn't dampen their spirits.

"It was really ironic, though. It was reverse, uh. . ." Nigel searches for the right word. "Reverse necrophilia, I guess. He was screwing us even in death."

The joyous feeling generated by the event nonetheless overflowed back at Nigel's nearby flat, where the three picked up acoustic guitars and played together for the first time in years. "I found myself," Derek says, "being drawn back to it like a moth to a fly."

And so, the tragic loss of Faith was the unexpected setting for Tap's resurrection. Asked about the irony, Derek nods sagely. "At this point, it's almost like we get more energy from adversity." Success, he opines, might tire them out. Could this, I wonder, be the much sought-after secret of Tap's incredible longevity?

"Psychologists have done studies finding that people who sail in smooth weather are very . . . bored," Nigel says sleepily. "And people who go in rough seas are—what?"

"Sharper," Derek says, adding sarcastically, "What, did *I* read the studies?"

Derek the headless bassman. (Photo by Sylvia Otte.)

I can't help thinking that these blokes have been together for so long that they can finish each other's sentences. I ask them if Derek, for instance, has ever been tempted to finish one of Nigel's solos on stage.

"That happened one night," Nigel says, "but no one could hear it, because the bass is so low. It's like with dog whistles."

After having been unceremoniously forced to flee Japan back in '82, Nigel hitchhiked across Europe and somehow managed to get inducted into the Swiss Army, an experience that seems to amuse more than rankle him when I ask about his days as a more-than-weekend warrior.

"The Swiss Army is very lovely as armies go," he says as we drive past a nightclub with a sign in the window offering $400 a week for male and female exotic dancers. "Somewhere between a scout troop and a school for waiters. They don't have any bullets in their guns. Don't print that, because they like to *think* they're frightening people—but they're *water* guns." Tufnel still has the Swiss Army knife he was given as a keepsake, and which he used as part of a special ecological unit that was sent out to cut the bark from trees and then repair them with bandages.

Before Switzerland, he'd swung down through various South Seas islands to "research different types of ethnic music. The islands I was working on are called the Pei Pei Islands," he says. "The Pei Pei people took me under their wing—they're not literally wings, they have arms like we do—and taught me all the rhythmic configurations they needed for me to know. Four-four is a joke to them; they have polyrhythms. They have polywogs as well."

"That's why it's called Polynesia," David chimes in.

Tufnel has also been busy with two new inventions: a folding wine glass for easy travel and something called an amp capo. The amp capo works on the same principle as the guitar capo, which changes the tuning of a guitar by sliding it up the neck. Nigel's much larger version is squeezed around the speaker cabinet of the amplifier and, as it's tightened by a struggling roadie, raises the pitch of the music being emitted. When I naively ask Nigel if the capo can help a standard amp go up to 11, like the ones he was so fond of in the DiBergi film, he arches a metaphorical eyebrow. "You're living in the Stone Age, aren't you? Eleven is a thing of the past. The new Marshalls go to 20, and *my* new system goes way past 20 anyway!"

He admits the folding wine glass has "a problem," though. The metal hinges work fine when it comes to folding, but the wine has a tendency to leak through after a few sips. "It does work better for the light wines. A Burgundy works, but the minute you get into a Bordeaux or an Italian wine, the sides start to fold down automatically."

It's getting late now, and the

band's new manager, Wendy Goldfinkel, is concerned that they haven't decided on a spot for the shoot. There's talk of a graveyard with monumental above-ground tombs—because of the swampy terrain, interment isn't feasible in the Big Easy—and the driver is instructed to head out there.

Meanwhile, Derek relates how he was stranded in Japan, having left his passport in a hotel room which no amount of hypnosis could help him to recall, and passed his days there "busking in the tube stations." This didn't prove popular, as the Japanese didn't take to his playing the bass. "It's not an instrument they have any sympathy with, because it's not part of their culture. Japanese music is all high, twangy instruments, and they don't really have a lot of bottom in anything they do."

After finally making it back to his home town of Nilford-on-Null, Smalls helped out with his ailing father's phone-sanitization business, and paid the rent by playing on some advertising jingles in London. His favorite was one for the Belgian Milk Board, which, translated roughly, went, "Milk—if it was any richer, it'd be cream!"

"It was very catchy in Flemish," Derek says.

Not catchy enough to keep Smalls from lunging at the chance to play real rock 'n' roll—even if it was for a band that "takes a different position towards the Supreme Evil One." He took over the bass slot with Christian rockers Lambsblood (their big hit was the crunching, Led Zep-influenced "Whole Lotta Lord"), when their bass player "backslid." His creative juices reactivated, Smalls responded by writing his longest composition in years, the seven-minute "SinBad Suite." But after two years of touring, he decided, he says, "to throw in my lot with evil again."

As we speed past the outskirts of town, St. Hubbins tells how he wound up in Los Angeles, where Jeanine "had put the down payment on a piece of property that turned out to be nonexistent." The story sends Nigel into a paroxysm of snickering and eyeball-rolling, which David ignores as he describes the "foothill community" of Pomona, 30 miles outside of L.A., where they rented a house while dealing with their legal hassles. "It just hit the spot with us, oh, rhythmically," he says. "We wound up warm in winter for the first time in our lives, and decided we'd like to stay." In search of American citizenship, David and Jeanine got married. "We hadn't read the booklet carefully enough, though. You know, that in order to get your green cards, at least one member of the marriage has to be an American citizen."

The experiment did pay dividends, however, as David discovered an unexpected domestic streak in his nature. He split his time between producing local garage bands and coaching the high school soccer team. Lacking formal training ("I've had no formal training in *anything*, now that you bring it up"), St. Hubbins finds that American youth respond to his coaching on the basis of his being English. "There's something about hearing it from the tongue of an Englishman that makes them think, 'Well, the

English *riot* when they don't like something. If they're not experts, at least they're hotheads, and we could certainly use a bit of that.'"

His local music productions included a group by the name of Diaperload. "We had to change that name, first of all," he says. "They're all tall and blond, so I just thought, Glam-rock. They went for it in a big way, and the group was rechristened Lamé. We thought it was a good name, except people kept leaving off that little accent mark. Now they're experimenting with the name Bumdummy. I still don't think it's quite the right move."

Meanwhile, drawing on her knowledge of fashion and the New Age, Jeanine started two shops. Her boutique offering the clothing of Ireland (mostly wool sweaters and assorted cold weather gear), called Potato Republic, hasn't quite caught on yet. "We don't have that natural market here in Southern California for big, thick, rough-hewn, itchy, woolly Irish sweaters," David explains. "It's just a matter of education, really." And then there's The Drippery, specializing in items of "vibrational significance" for the New Age, such as herb candles, which have "little pockets of medicinal liquids within the candles that are released upon their exposure to the air."

Recent publicity photos of St. Hubbins show him in a variety of outfits, from musketeer regalia to primitive buckskin, leading to speculation that Jeanine has been "channeling" characters from the past. David dismisses the notion, even as he cranes his neck to get a look at the Voodoo Museum the limo is just passing. He explains that, for a while, Jeanine was seeing a woman who claimed to be channeling the spirit of Louis Armstrong—until she caught the same woman performing in a club as a professional mimic. "She was doing Cagney and Barbra Streisand, so Jeanine doesn't really believe in the channeling thing anymore. No, I've been experimenting with fantasy characters, figures from literature," he says, fingering the blue brocade of an Edwardian vest he's wearing today.

Jeanine got the inspiration for it all from reading romance novels. "When we first met, one of the things that struck Jeanine was that I was very similar—psychically and rhythmically rather than in looks, of course—to a samurai warrior that she had been involved with in the late 15th century. I think that the past is overlooked as a source for the present. Rather than look for the next big thing, I like getting all retro." Much as David savors the buckskin look, however, he admits it's difficult to get around in. "It's very fresh buckskin, so it's got a layer of fatty tissue on the inside. That's a bit squishy, and rather noisy. But once we get it properly cured, I'll be making more use of it."

Back in the present-day world, *Break Like the Wind* unquestionably sets a new standard in production values for Spinal Tap, replacing the band's accustomed lumbering tracks with a spiffy new verve. With guest producers of the caliber of Danny Kortchmar (Bon Jovi), Steve Lukather (Toto, Cher), Dave Jerden and T-Bone Burnett, guitar solos contributed by everyone from Jeff Beck and

Slash (of Guns N' Roses) to Joe Satriani and Dweezil Zappa, and a guest vocal by Cher (on the Smalls-penned power ballad, "Just Begin Again"), the album has the feel of an all-star production. Question is, has the band lost that scruffy edge of primitive naivete that lent them what appeal they once had? In short, has Spinal Tap sold out? A sudden silence fills the limo after I put it to them bluntly: Are you just going for the money this time around?

David is the first to open up. "We were going for the money *every* time around," he says, toying with the voluminous ruffles on his white lace shirt. "We are first and foremost commercial salesmen, selling rock 'n' roll. No shame in that— the shame comes when no one buys it."

"If people shove money in our faces . . ." Nigel begins. "We'll take it," Derek completes his thought.

Nigel nods solemnly. "Well, first we'll say, 'Don't put it in my face, put it in my hand.' But yeah, we'll take it."

"If we'd gone the other way and said we're just going to do another old Spinal Tap album and we don't want any help, thank you," Derek adds, straightening a thickly studded leather wristband, "people would've said, 'Well, they're stuck in the Seventies.'"

"You can't get round it," Nigel says. "Someone's always going to have a theory about what we're doing, and in this case it's that we've gone commercial. But why don't they say that about Cher? They could say, 'Cher,

you're using Tap to, like, tie yourself to a rocket.'"

Indeed, there's a revealing story behind the Cher guest spot. The band felt they needed a special kind of duet for the power ballad, "and Howard Keel didn't seem right for the part." That's where Steve Lukather came in handy. Besides having produced Cher's last album, he also had some candid photographs of the singer to hold over her head. A quick call from Lukather, according to Smalls, and Cher was calling the band, "*begging* to be on the track."

About those photos—did they depict Cher in some compromising situation? "Oh, very compromising," Derek adds. "I've never seen the photos, but Steve says that she's wearing, like, Peter Pan blouses and turtleneck sweaters, business suits, penny loafers, things she'd be totally embarrassed to have shown in public."

The band is quick to refute feminist accusations that their new single, "Bitch School," is demeaning to women (much the way, eight years ago, they'd bristled at accusations that the cover of their *Smell the Glove* LP was sexist rather than, as they insisted, merely sexy). To be sure, the lyrics *are* provocative: "You got problems/You whine and you beg/When I'm busy/You wanna dance with my leg/I'm gonna chain you/Make you sleep out of doors/You're so fetching when you're down on all fours."*

*Lyrics Copyright 1992 by MCA Music Publishing, a division of MCA Music Inc. and Discharge Music (ASCAP). Used by permission. All rights reserved.

"If you have half a brain in your head," Nigel says in a tone dripping with *Weltschmertz,* "you can see it's about dog training. The end. Period. Question mark. Exclamation point. Hyphen. I mean, what fetches on all fours?"

"It's about instilling habits of obedience into our canine friends," Derek says.

"You can take any bloody pop song and twist it around," Nigel continues. "Take a song like 'Norwegian Wood.' If you grew up in England you'd know that that's a euphemism for an erection. But in this country that got misinterpreted, and now the same thing's happened to us." The scads of scantily clad women in the video of "Bitch School" were the record company's idea—an idea that Tap went along with nevertheless. "When we were young and arrogant," Smalls explains, "we'd say, 'No, it's about dogs, so only dogs in the video.'"

"But we've matured," says David.

The limo has arrived at the graveyard, which, with its ranks of towering marble and limestone mausoleums, is genuinely awe-inspiring. The sun is close to setting as the band looks around, shuddering involuntarily. The photographer feels the locale will suit the band's image, what with their horned death's head logo, but the lads aren't so sure. "This boneyard gives me the willies," Nigel announces, to nods all around. It has become clear to all involved that the band who had modest hits with "Have a Nice Death" and "Christmas with the Devil" are not about to set foot in a ceme-

tery, even in daylight. Finally, the limo begins to proceed to the front gates, and the mood inside lightens considerably. Derek has an idea for a new Spinal Tap movie. "It's a horror film," he says rubbing his hands gleefully. "All the dead drummers come back to life!"

It's no secret in the music world that Tap look on the Marty DiBergi documentary, which nonetheless made them household names in America, as another kind of horror movie. "It's a hatchet job," says Nigel, his chin dimpling in anger. DiBergi, he argues, chose to show "only the things that go wrong." Derek points out that during performances of "Rock and Roll Creation," he gets out of the transparent plastic pod "sixty to eighty per cent of the time, easy." And he adds, "You see us being portrayed playing on the stage in Cleveland. But do you ever see us *finding* the stage? No, you only see us *not* finding the stage. It's just common sense we had to have found the stage, isn't it? But he doesn't show that. He loads the dice, and then refuses to throw them."

It reminds Nigel of the movie *Who's Afraid of Virginia Woolf?* "Imagine how embarrassed Liz Taylor was to see her marriage portrayed like that," he says.

Across the limo, David is nodding his head as he pours himself a sizable drink from the well-stocked bar, and passes the bottle around.

"You might have gotten the impression from seeing the film that we were sort of doomed, and that's not what it was like at all. It was an average, semi-

successful album promotion tour, nothing more, nothing less."

Even when nobody showed up at their in-store record signing?

"Again, it was one of those things that happen," David insists with a dismissive wave. "It turned out that Jack Nicklaus was autographing his golf album in a store right down the block, and we just happened to have concurrent markets."

Wendy Goldfinkel announces from the front seat that, as darkness has set in, they'll have to put off the photo shoot for another day. The Tap triumvirate hardly raise a collective eyebrow. For all their sense of constant betrayal, the band seems to have learned to take these little setbacks in stride. Their new mantra, repeated often throughout the interview, is "We've matured." Like when their plans to outdo Springsteen and Guns N' Roses by releasing *three* CDs simultaneously fell through after the masters for the second and third albums disappeared under "suspicious" circumstances. Or like that absurdly late soundcheck earlier this morning.

"In the old days," Nigel says with a naughty, nostalgic gleam in his eye, "we would have walked out *and* destroyed the place. But we didn't do either."

David confesses that they *did* pull apart one guitar stand "as a sort of controlled experiment in temper, rather than a tantrum." Nigel's jaw has fallen in a familiar pout, and for the first time today he looks the least bit steamed.

"You see, that bit was stolen," he says, controlling himself. He tells me that during the mid-Sixties, Tap played a festival with The Who. "They saw us destroy our guitar stands. We used to take 'em and smash 'em during our shows."

Just the stands?

"Well, yeah. We couldn't afford to smash the *instruments*. A few years later, they, of course, had made some money, and they started destroying their guitars. Where do you suppose *that* came from?"

Derek wonders aloud why Marty DiBergi didn't put stories like that one in his so-called rockumentary. "He had an axe to grind, because he says to himself, How am I gonna make more money? By just showing a hard-working band slogging through the road, or by making them look like blithering yobbos?"

There are nods of agreement all around as the limo speeds off into the night. "People come up to us and ask, 'Are you gonna get out of the pod tonight?'" Derek adds with a tone of genuine hurt. "Or, 'Have you figured out how big Stonehenge should be yet?' It makes us a laughing stock."

The diminutive bassist reflects for a moment, his eyes vibrant as if gazing finally into the heart of the matter. "David put it best when he said, 'People who see that movie might never dream that we're really a smooth band.'"

Taken from *Metalsounds*, April 1992

TAPPING AN AMERICAN VEIN: A BAND FOR OUR (HARD) TIMES

by Howie Weinberger

The economy sucks, the infrastructure is rotting faster than last week's pizza, and the only thing you have to look forward to in the morning is the trip to your mailbox. So why Spinal Tap? Why now? Who needs another heavy metal band with more Marshall amps than Blue Cheer, more Spandex than brains, and more songs in their long, checkered past than they can remember the lyrics to?

Okay, I'll tell you why.

In case you thought you had to suffer all alone, left high and dry by the receding waves of economic growth like some beached whale, Spinal Tap lets you know they're down in the trenches with you, grounded in everyday problems—namely, struggling to keep that next gig from being canceled. Indeed, few bands have proven as resilient, as pliable even, as Spinal Tap. Few have so often risen Phoenix-like from the ashes of previous débâcles and suddenly dying drummers, or survived so many failed attempts to catch that just-

departed bandwagon of a once-profitable musical trend, and lived to play another day. In fact, Tap's genius for retooling their few genuine hits of past days to match their latest sound represents an economy of means that our bloated American industrialists could well learn from.

None of which would amount to a hill of Hell Holes, of course, without the music. And the words—let's not forget the words. But to understand Tap the phenomenon, we have to dig back into the dustbin of their past. To understand where they're going, we have to first find out where they're coming from.

Maybe it all began to take shape for Tap when Neil "Tonedeath" Witherspoon wrote his first rave review in London's *Metalsounds* magazine in 1974. That was the one in which he likened David St. Hubbins and his raging mane of blond locks to "a charlady who's fallen down on stage and can't get back up, and is waving

her mop frantically above her supine body in a futile plea for help!" Reputations are made of less vibrant images than that. There have been other characterizations along the way, too, like "savage stampede of butchering buccaneers," "muscle-bound melodies," "historical histrionics," and, naturally, "one of Britain's loudest bands." But the image of a man flat on his rear end, striving futilely to get back on his feet again (and looking damn foolish in the process)—that's what Spinal Tap is all about. That's why we keep sneaking back for more.

A reference to the past, to their early formative days, is no accident, either. Listening to Tap today can be, as Joe Franklin might put it, like a trip down memory lane. For openers, there's "Majesty of Rock" from their latest LP, *Break Like The Wind* (MCA/Dead Faith), with its faint whiff of the early-Eighties British freak band Specimen's "The Beauty of Poison." Or the echoes of early Steppenwolf crossed with Moby Grape in

"Springtime." Or the compendium of Merseybeat-cum-psychedelia in "Rainy Day Sun." Tap is nothing if not the palimpsest of rock history.

Having said that, I hardly mean to undervalue their ability to ring significant, if marginal, changes on other bands' work, to wring the last drop of vestigially marketable product out of what might have seemed like an already dead horse, to mix metaphors just a bit.

Because there's more. There's the "serious" side of Tap—and I don't just mean Nigel's abiding affection for Mozart! Their songs are consistently filled with the finely observed details of which serious art is constructed, as in these lines from "Stinking Up the Great Outdoors" on *Break Like The Wind*:

Ain't nothin' like a festival crowd
There's too many people so we play too loud. *

Don't get me wrong. I don't presume to tar these boys with the same brush so often used to denigrate the self-consciously pretentious art-rock of decades past (eat your heart out, David Byrne!). It's just that Spinal Tap never fail to tell it like it is, even if they have to bear (good-naturedly) some of the brunt themselves:

The lights are bullshit, the sound's for the birds
Don't know the music, and we don't know the words
Now we're stinking up the great outdoors . . .
But the kids don't mind. *

"Why waste good music on a brain?" (Photo by Sylvia Otte.)

And just because their forte is portraying, in all its banal simplicity, the unembellished grit of everyday rock and roll life, that doesn't mean the great songwriting team of Tufnel–St. Hubbins isn't sometimes capable of high wit. "And that's the majesty of rock, the mystery of roll," they sing in "Majesty of Rock," and then the images come tumbling crazily by like so much brightly colored laundry glimpsed through the porthole of a whirling front-loader at the local coin-op:

The darning of a sock
The scoring of the goal
The farmer takes a wife
The barber takes a pole. *

(Or is it "takes a poll"—how's that for ambiguity?) But all this pungent delirium would mean nothing if Tap couldn't deliver the megatonnage to moor their wildest whimsy in the solid concrete of good ol' proletarian thump and drone. And when it comes to concrete, no bigger bunch of bottom-heavy, slow-drying, stick-your-foot-in-it-at-your-own-risk chord churners ever slashed a path across the overgrown jungles of God's all-too-green earth than the men of Spinal Tap. You want Heavy Duty? They got it:

Clockwise from left: Ice, Fire, Lukewarm Water. (Photo by Sylvia Otte.)

No light fantastic ever crosses my mind
That meditation stuff can make you go blind
Just crank that volume to the point of pain
Why waste good music on a brain?†

Why, indeed?

And did I hear someone out there question Tap's work ethic? Guess again. This is, after all, the band whose output was once described by that great champion of plebeian pop, Dave Marsh, as "A style, indeed a

universe, of rock music so tough, gritty, and grungy in its delivery that only success can justify their hard work." Or words to that effect.

The really remarkable thing is that Tap have achieved what success they have without the conventional scenario of favorable critical reviews, overwhelming popular support, massive record sales, and all the other accoutrements that have made life so easy for the great bands of rock. No, the men of Tap have done it all mostly by dint of their own, well, persistence.

So then who, as the Hindus might ask, are these manifest-

ations of the Rock 'n' Roll Godhead? Let's take a closer look at the individuals of Tap.

As Derek Smalls himself so astutely noted in the tantalizingly selective "rockumentary" *This Is Spinal Tap*, Nigel and David represent the opposing poles of "fire and ice" to his moderating "lukewarm water." And so they are: fire and ice, yin and yang (actually, yang and yin), pepper and salt, bubble and squeak, gin and tonic. For as much as Nigel may admire his beloved Mozart, it's David who is the Apollonian figure in this rock triumvirate. Nigel, of course, is pure post-rational Dionysian demiurge, not so much beyond logic as completely outside it. For Señor Tufnel, life is not a conundrum but a child's toy—one of those little glass globes with synthetic snowflakes inside that, no matter which way you turn it, is always aswirl in new vistas, new images, new planes of Being, new ... what? OK, I may have gotten in over my head on this metaphor. Let's move along.

On to Derek, for instance: the cerebral center of the band. Don't let the leather harness and chest hair fool you; his reference points are Shelley and Byron. No tweed-jacketed dweeb but a real thinking man's thinker, Smalls may well be the linch-pin of the whole operation, the sane middle ground that anchors the excesses of his more exuberant line-mates. It's not for nothing, after all, that he plays the bass.

If David and Nigel, then, represent the eternal adolescent, Derek is maturity in youth, the

Wise Old Man in each of us, no matter how young at heart. Tap's complementary personae are even apparent in the photos that grace their new CD: David in classic Lone Muscateer attire, all lace and fenching foil; Nigel swathed in space-age leathers, the Bacchanalian Biker par excellence; and Derek, dear old Derek, still the leather-and-studs man at heart, a Rocker of Ages in a sea of change. I don't think it is stretching the point too far to say that, together, they form a rock 'n' roll Trinity capable of servicing the spiritual needs of a whole generation.

And now Spinal Tap has once again resurrected itself from incipient obscurity and reemerged from what may be their most challenging near-death experience ever, enlightened by new visions of the Rock 'n' Roll Beyond. If those visions have less to do with tunnels of blue light and more to do with making piles of green this time around, well, then, that's just another way in which Spinal Tap reflect the workaday realities around them. Barometer of the times that they are, they are once more showing us the way to survival in perilous

times: persistence amid great indifference, triumph amid deep mediocrity, and an uncanny ability to retrofit old hardware with new software at minimal expense.

So if, as Shirley MacLaine has suggested, it's now a time for "Going Within," why not let Spinal Tap show us the way? We could do a lot worse, couldn't we?

Taken from *Infotainment Today*, March 22, 1992

THEY REMEMBER SPINAL TAP

As part of the 25th Anniversary of Spinal Tap's formation, Jeanine Pettibone-St. Hubbins and Mike Pym, two characters who wouldn't seem to have very much in common were it not for their link to Spinal Tap, were asked to offer their earliest reminiscences of the band. The results, I think you'll agree, are as different as oil and water.

Spinal Tap, David, and me
A Very Personal View
by Jeanine Pettibone-St. Hubbins

The Moments That Matter in the lives we lead stand out like jutting cliffs along the shoreline of Memory . . .

I am at a party. My friend Detmer's flat. The music is Coltrane, all rage, lust and Godhead. I am throwing the *I Ching* for poor Rutger, dead that very morning of botulism. The coins seem possessed of an outside force other than their usual cosmic spin. Odd. Rather like TV interference when someone walks through the room wearing aluminum clothing. An Entity. I turned . . .

The shock of blond . . . the blaze of red velvet . . . the aura of Remy Martin . . . and Something Else. This pale creature is more than he seems, surely—and all at once it comes to me! The Shogun! The Dream Warrior I had known in my slumbers for so many years, truly made flesh,

clearly Reborn in the guise of a moderately well-known pop figure! What girl could ask for more?

And so it came to pass: the 700-year-old dead Japanese Warrior-Poet and the 645-year-old dead Japanese Princess (me) became as One. Or, counting the rest of the band, Six. And we've had our ups and downs, our Yins and Yangs, to be sure. But my association with Spinal Tap has been more than just physical; I feel my soul linked to this incredible group and their mighty works rather like a string links a sky-bound kite to the ancient Earth. They are Fantasy that will not be tamed. I am Reality that will not be denied.

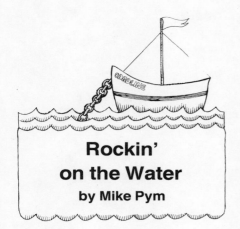

Rockin' on the Water
by Mike Pym

They entered the studio unsteadily, as if the pitching and rolling of the ship were making them nauseous (which it turned out to be doing). I was hosting the late-night program on Radio Caroline,and the wobbly-legged members of Spinal Tap had been brought out to the pirate ship in a record-company-leased skiff to promote "(Listen to the) Flower People."

Nigel seemed a dark and brooding lad, the obligatory shock of shiny hair covering a dour Cockney countenance. Derek was harder to read, rolling and smoking a variety of joints the history of whose contents he insisted on detailing, like an oddly bewhiskered wine steward. David was, as ever, the dreamer, the poet, the one who actually seemed to believe there were flower children and that we should in fact listen to them.

When the leased skiff headed back early, delaying the lads' return to land by a day, we struck up a friendship nourished by their need for some place (namely, my cabin) in which to enjoy a modicum of privacy whilst they returned their respective lunches to sender.

In the years to come, as yours truly migrated shoreward and took up his perch as host of the longest-running needle-drop-and-live-performance program on British medium-wave radio, the Tappers would visit our studios whenever they had a new record to promote. As our engineers struggled to cope with their increasing loudness, you could see the band growing into their style, using volume as, if you will, a fourth chord.

Their twin obsessions—sex and history—manifested themselves in increasingly elaborate lyrical inventions. Meantime, Nigel's fretwork eluded his peers and showed what, all that time back, he had been brooding about.

Today, our program is recorded on digital tape, and we are soon to become the first all-hard-disk radio show on medium wave. As I look back on the literally hundreds of bands who've come into our studio and made the case for their music, no band's contribution seems as persistent—nay, as stubborn in its refusal to bow to popular negation—as that of these three dogged musical warriors and their confreres on the back line. If it's hard for you to believe that it's been twenty-five years since Spinal Tap first assaulted your aural cavities, imagine how I feel.

If it takes twenty-five more years for these fellows to get into the Rock 'N' Roll Hall of Fame, put your money on Tap, if not for their sonic crunch and lyrical ambiguity, just for their brute persistence. And don't tell them I said so, but this time, I just might play their record, too.

(Mike Pym hosts "Pym's Cup", the first and still the only British pop show in AM stereo.)

R.I.P.

John "Stumpy" Pepys

Eric "Stumpy Joe" Childs

Peter "James" Bond

Mick Shrimpton

Joe "Mama" Besser

Richard ("Ric") Shrimpton

THEY DIED BEFORE THEY GOT OLD: A CONCISE GUIDE TO SPINAL TAP'S DRUMMERS

Name	Dates	Cause of Death
John "Stumpy" Pepys	(1943–1969)	*Gardening accident*

NIGEL: "I really rescued Johnny from a lifetime which would have been spent in the mines in England."
DEREK: "Yeah, but it would have been a *lifetime*."
DAVID: "He was a bit older than we were, but he looked a lot younger. He was like my younger big brother."

Eric "Stumpy Joe" Childs	(1945–1974)	*Choked on vomit*

DEREK: "Big hands, big feet, big heart. Small lips. Thin hair. Big ears. That really says it all. I mean, you could use that to make a police sketch of him."
DAVID: "A very natural drummer. He was sort of the ascetic, the eremite, the mystic drummer, the most connected to the rhythms of the universe. Of course, we didn't have these catch phrases around then, but that's how I remember him."

Peter "James" Bond   (1949–1977)   *Spontaneous combustion*

DAVID: "The ultimate professional. Snappy dresser. The only member of this band ever to wear a tie on a regular basis."

NIGEL: "For a drummer, he had very good time. He could actually keep the rhythm pretty much in the ballpark, as you would say, for the whole tune. His death really hit me the hardest, because he owed me money."

DEREK: "As the bass player, I work most closely with the drummer. We really have to become almost an extension of ourselves in each other. I would say he's a riddle wrapped in something very obvious."

Mick Shrimpton   (1948–1982)   *Onstage explosion*

DAVID: "Mick was a substance abuser, and he was constantly seeking new substances to abuse. Once he hit upon one he'd say, 'Oh, here's·one—this'll bring me to the brink of death.' I don't know whether that had anything to do with his ultimate explosion, but he was not a healthy individual."

NIGEL: "He was just so sweet, everyone loved him. He never showed up on time but you still had to love him because he was the essence of a Tap drummer: he was fearless."

DEREK: "Mick was like, when your dog makes a mess, and you want to hit him, and you want to love him, and you want to clean it up, all at once. It's a handful. The way I like to think of it is, he's up there in heaven showing up late every day."

NIGEL: "He's probably not even there yet. He's calling and saying his car broke down."

Joe "Mama" Besser   (19??–1983)   *Missing, presumed dead*

DAVID: "The largest member of this band, ever. He got bored if he had to play 4/4 for more than a few measures in a row, so he was always slipping into 7/8 and all these strange time signatures. After the gig he would fall into a meditative state, his heartbeat would slow down virtually to nothing, and we had the roadies carry him out. He was a big bloke, so they had to use a ramp to get him down off the drum riser. After the Japan débâcle, we ended up putting a lot of stuff in storage, and we're not quite sure where the building was. So Joe might still be in with the rest of the equipment. In which case we might as well kiss him goodbye."

NIGEL: "He wasn't just a big fat bastard—I mean, he was a lot more than that. He could play almost anything. Unfortunately, he chose to play almost *nothing* when you wanted him to play *everything*, or vice versa.

DEREK: On the other hand, he'd play almost *anything* when you wanted him to play *something*.

Richard ("Ric") Shrimpton   (1948–   )   *Still living . . .*

NIGEL: "Believe me, Rick knows the full story, we're not keeping anything from him. I don't know if I'd say he has a great future ahead of him. He's got a *limited* future, but it may be great."

DEREK: "He's got a great *present* ahead of him, let's put it that way."

DAVID: "He still runs 20 to 30 minutes late for rehearsal, but for a drummer that's very conscientious. Counting all the session men and temporaries, he is our 13th drummer. But don't tell *him* that—he'll be worried sick. I think that 13 is a lucky number in his case. As long as he keeps from urinating on the third rail or something, he should last a long time."

TAP ALIVE:
SPINAL TAP
on "SATURDAY
NIGHT LIVE"

The Men of Tap.

The following is a verbatim transcript of an excerpt from Spinal Tap's appearance on "Saturday Night Live" in May 1984, as originally broadcast over the NBC Television Network.

BARRY BOSTWICK: So tell me, what has your week been like on "Saturday Night Live"?

NIGEL TUFNEL: Well, it's very excitin' doin' a live show—

DAVID ST. HUBBINS: It's a whirlwind of activity.

TUFNEL: We don't get that many calls—the last one was in 'sixty . . . eight.

DEREK SMALLS: I think what we really value about it is the *honesty,* y'know, of just goin' out there naked with our guts spread out in front of the tube and sayin', y'know, there's no fake, there's nothing, there's no *tape*—

ST. HUBBINS: You can't fake guts. You can't fake guts when they're laid out like that.

TUFNEL: It's a great idea. Y'know, here we are in front of all these, y'know, what? It must be like three hundred thousand people watching, or something—

ST. HUBBINS: Twenty million, on Saturday night, easy.

TUFNEL: Really?

ST. HUBBINS: That's what the man said. Twenty million.

TUFNEL: Cor* . . . Well, the great thing about it is that,

Cor is a rough transliteration of an unintelligible Cockney expletive.—Ed.

y'know, you get up there and you go, "We're gonna play loud," and they go, "Yeah...."

ST. HUBBINS: It's marvelous—

TUFNEL: What would they say? It's live, what could they say?

ST. HUBBINS: They can't say, "Stop that!"

SMALLS: They can't say, "Sorry...."

TUFNEL: They can't say [rubs index fingers together], "No, no, no loud."

ST. HUBBINS: Too late.

TUFNEL: They can't do that. Then we go, "Too late for you."

ST. HUBBINS: Yeah, it's a great feeling. It's a feeling of... [He sneezes; jump-cut to St. Hubbins now smoking a cigarette.] But, it's really like a feeling of power you get, y'know, when it's live like that.

TUFNEL: Yeah.

SMALLS: Yeah.

BOSTWICK: Why do you play so loud?

TUFNEL: It's like in the old days, y'know, a lot of people say, y'know, Well, Mozart, he didn't play loud. Well, that's a lot of, uh, bullwhack, y'know?

ST. HUBBINS: It's rubbish.

TUFNEL: He played as loud as he could. And if he'd had an amp, if he'd turned it up, he would've been able to, but he didn't have it, y'know.

ST. HUBBINS: And he was sort of really deaf... y'know it's not like—

SMALLS & TUFNEL: No, that was Beethoven.

ST. HUBBINS: Oh.

TUFNEL: No, but Mozart, when he played—he played keyboards —he would put his ear down to the uh, soundboard and, y'know, really jam it *in* there. Y'know, *smash* it. And his mom would go, "Mozart! Mozart! Don't play loud!" But he would anyway.

BOSTWICK: Who do you think your music appeals to?

TUFNEL: Um, I say... professionals. People who work as professionals in the business: you know, a neurosurgeon... y'know—

SMALLS: Stockbrokers—

TUFNEL: Stockbrokers... Businessmen who are serious about life.

SMALLS: Investment bankers ... serious people.

TUFNEL: Yeah, serious... trilateral commission, those type of people.

ST. HUBBINS: Illuminati, uh, and fourteen-year-old *white* boys.

BOSTWICK: Ah, you're doing a song on the show called "Christmas with the Devil." Are you seriously interested in devil worship, or are you just using the trappings of Satanism to get attention?

ST. HUBBINS: I personally feel that it's an important thing, well, what you were saying the other day [turns to Smalls]...

SMALLS: Well, it's basically a matter of, y'know, I believe, and I think it goes for everybody in the band, that a man's relationship with the devil is a very private affair, y'know. It's not something you wear about on your sleeve. We're not doin' it to, y'know, put up billboards and say, "Oh, look, we're Satanists—"

TUFNEL: We're not rushin' about the streets, y'know, flingin' our hats about, sayin', "Oh, I love Satan, he's my master...."

SMALLS: "Look at me—"

TUFNEL: Yeah, "Look at me, Mr. Satanism..." Y'know, *sure* it's great stuff... sure—

ST. HUBBINS: And it's excitin'.

TUFNEL: *And* it's excitin'... and—

SMALLS: And it's dangerous.

TUFNEL: *And* it's danger—it has a danger to it. But, y'know, you don't hang your whole life on it. It's just part of what we do.

SMALLS: It's an evening—it's an evening's fun.

TUFNEL: Y'know, in terms of history, the devil was really the master of all. And Christmas— the original Christmas ceremony —was a devil, runnin' about with his tail, his little red tail... And y'know, he would have this little fork on the end of his tail, and he'd go, "You stay away from here, it's Christmas," poke, poke [gestures with hand as if holding tail]. He would do that, y'know, that was really the basis....

SMALLS: So we're takin' it back 'round where it started, y'know.

People think, Well you're twisting Christmas, or something like that, but . . .

ST. HUBBINS: It was originally a heathen rite.

TUFNEL: Sure.

BOSTWICK: Some of your songs, like "Big Bottom," seem to portray women as sex objects, not as human beings. How do you feel about that?

ST. HUBBINS: Well, that's interesting, you know, because I think it's important, I think we should underline this: It's important that we do *not* consider the subject of this song a human being at all but merely *part* of one. Therefore, that gives us sort of a license to, like, be as free as we want without really worrying about whose feelings we hurt. There are no feelings involved here at all.

TUFNEL: Yeah, no, it's not like we're saying women are this or women are that. We are merely making, if you like, a scientific study of the bun.

ST. HUBBINS: And its ultimate—

TUFNEL: Rendition.

ST. HUBBINS: —rendition.

SMALLS: And it's odd, y'know, because the nature of the song is a *tribute* to a large, uh—

ST. HUBBINS: Keister.

SMALLS: —pair o' cheeks, y'know, and it's not about a woman at all.

ST. HUBBINS: No.

SMALLS: It's about a woman's pair o' cheeks. And it's like sayin', Oh, because you wrote a song about a woman's nose, then you're not respectin' her as a person. It's about a *nose!*

TUFNEL: I mean, no one would say, if, y'know, you wrote it about a gent's bum. . . . They'd say, Well, so what?

SMALLS: Good work, they'd say.

TUFNEL: They say, Good luck to *you*, I hope it goes up the charts.

SMALLS: I'll bet he had it comin' to him, they'd say.

TUFNEL: Yeah. And if it's about a young lady, suddenly: "Ooooh, naughtynaughty on you!" So what's that all about?

BOSTWICK [to the audience]: Now, ladies and gentlemen, this was to have been their Christmas 1983 release, but apparently studio time was all booked up through the first of the year. So, well, here they are, celebrating Christmas in May . . . Spinal Tap! ["Christmas with the Devil" is performed live.]

"CHRISTMAS WITH THE DEVIL"

The elves are dressed in leather
And the angels are in chains
   Christmas with the Devil

The sugar plums are rancid
And the stockings are in flames
   Christmas with the Devil
There's a demon in my belly
And a gremlin in my brain
There's someone up the chimney hole
And Satan is his name

The rats ate all the presents
And the reindeer ran away
   Christmas with the Devil

There'll be no Father Christmas
'Cause it's Evil's holiday
   Christmas with the Devil
No bells in Hell
No show below
Silent night, violent night . . .

So come all ye unfaithful
Don't be left out in the cold
You don't need no invitation
Your ticket is your soul

The elves are dressed in leather
And the angels are in chains
The sugar plums are rancid
And the stockings are in flames
   Christmas with the Devil
   Christmas with the Devil
   [Repeat eight times and fade.]

[Spoken]
This is Spinal Tap, wishing you and yours
the most joyous of holiday seasons.
God bless us, everyone.
   Christmas with the Devil*

Performing "Christmas with the Devil" on SNL.
(Collection of the author.)

*Words and music by Spinal Tap.
© 1984 Scary Music.
Reproduced by permission. All rights reserved.

AFTERTHOUGHT: TUFNEL on TAP on SNL

"Well, I didn't see
the show, y'see.
I just *heard* about it.
It was live, y'know,
so you can't *watch* it
while you're doin' it."

A NOTE OF WARNING

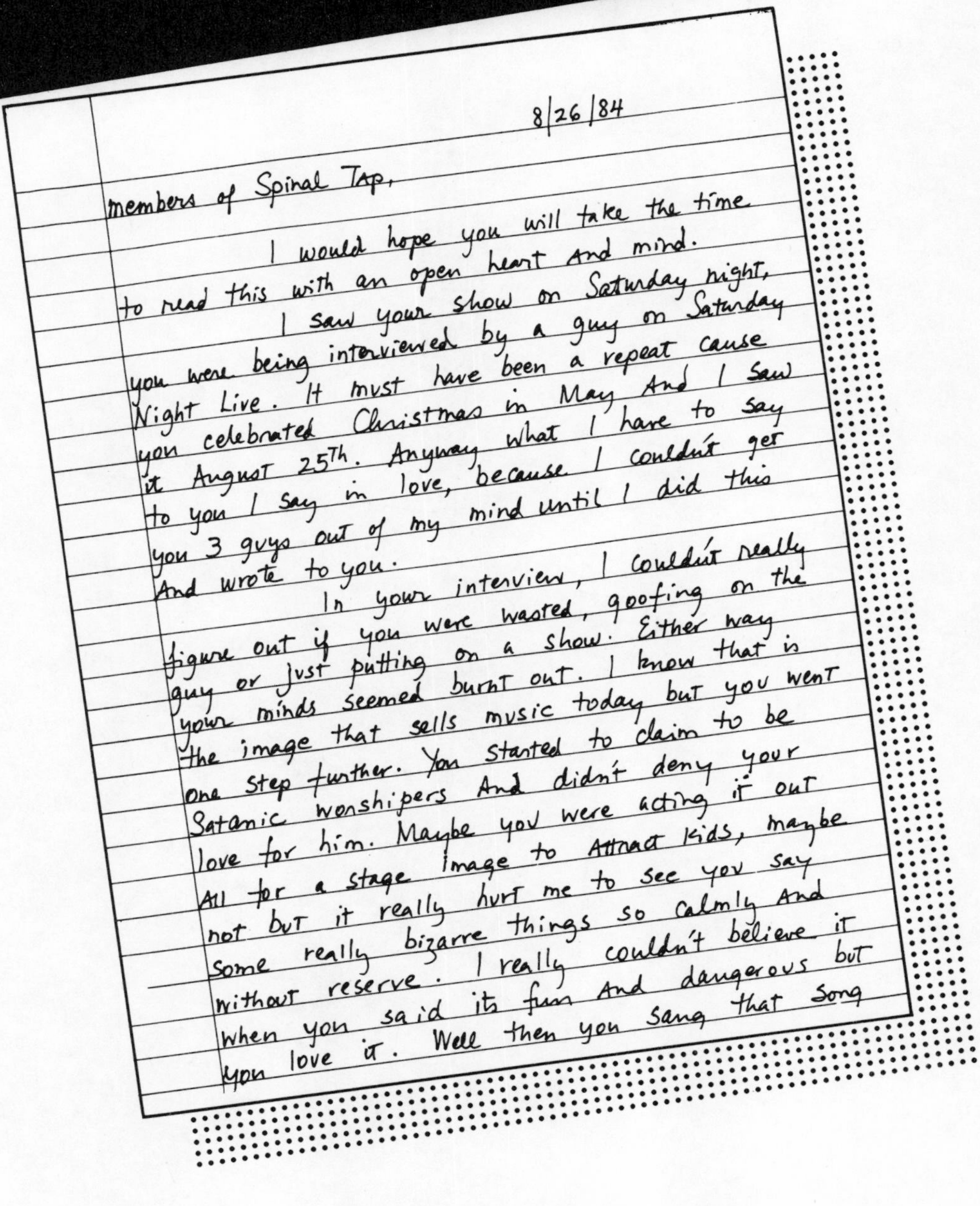

8/26/84

members of Spinal Tap,

    I would hope you will take the time to read this with an open heart And mind.
    I saw your show on Saturday night, you were being interviewed by a guy on Saturday Night Live. It must have been a repeat cause you celebrated Christmas in May And I saw it August 25th. Anyway what I have to say to you I say in love, because I couldn't get you 3 guys out of my mind until I did this And wrote to you.
    In your interview, I couldn't really figure out if you were wasted, goofing on the guy or just putting on a show. Either way your minds seemed burnt out. I know that is the image that sells music today but you went one step further. You started to claim to be Satanic worshipers And didn't deny your love for him. Maybe you were acting it out All for a stage image to Attract kids, maybe not but it really hurt me to see you say some really bizarre things so Calmly And without reserve. I really couldn't believe it when you said its fun And dangerous but you love it. Well then you sang that song

After saying the Devil had the original Christmas. I heard the first chorus About someone in Leather, Angels in chains Christmas with the devil.

In all honesty I had had dreams all night and woke up with you guys on my mind. My spirit hurt so bad to see you so very deceived.

You see, whether you know it or not, everytime you open yourself up to demonic worship or even joke about it, it really isn't a joke! You may not really believe what I'm gonna say but it's God's truth. Satan is as real as God is, That has always been true. And he's Always tried to imitate And try to be God. That is why he is a fallen Angel today. He still to this day tries to ACT like God and deceive those who open themselves up To his evil power. He isn't the guy in red with horns and a pitchfork, the bible tells us he is an angel of light And he would try to deceive Jesus himself if he could. It also says he is a roaring lion going about seeing whom he may devour. And it also says to resist the devil And he will flee from you.

You see Satan knows that Jesus has

come here to save men's souls, his death was to shed his perfect sinless blood for All who would Ask for it. When Jesus was in the grave Satan thought Wow he's gone. I win. But thank God that Jesus rose, And the bible says that he know has the keys to death Hell + the grave. He has won the spiritual fight. The Devil knows this he also knows the ending of the story. Read revelations in the Bible. He is beat. But being a real sly guy. He figures as long as he's going to hell, he might as well take along As many As he can.

Please — Don't believe him. The Bible calls him the father of lies, the deceiver, the Father of lust. Whatever is Against God that is what he is for. And even if you do all this for a gimmick, its more dangerous than you'll ever know. eternity is A LONG Time, And believe me when Satan gets someone to hell, he will laugh at you forever And he wont have favorites or followers. You will all be in torment together. Its not worth the money to play this music, Its not worth eternity for A few years here. The Bible Also says, what does it profit a man/ if he gains the whole world yet looses his soul. Jesus ! the giver of life. Satan is the taker of souls And life. All his powers on earth all, his deceiving will one day come to an end And where will that leave you. You may not believe a word of this. But I am going to pray for you because it is that importanT And Christ in me loves you And hurts for you.

You probably know alot about the devil so let me tell you how God feels about you. He loves you, yes even now in your sin. the Bible says. For God so loved the world that he gave his only son so that whosoever shall believe in him will have everlasting life. For Jesus did not come into this world to be its judge but to be its savior. John 3:16

Also he says - I Am the way - the truth And the life - no man comes to the father but by me. John.

If you believe with your heart And confess with your mouth that Jesus Christ is Lord you shall be saved. Romans.

I feel better now knowing that I listened to God and wrote you this letter, he loves you so very much, And because he loves you. I can love you with his perfect love.

Please feel free to write me And share your feelings. I will be praying for you. And even if you hate me or what I have said, its ok. Cause he will still love you. And so will I, you can't deny the perfect grace And unconditional love of God.

God Bless.
Love in Christ
Peggy Sutcliffe
66 Maple Drive
Pompton Plains, N.J.
07444

My husband also will pray for you.

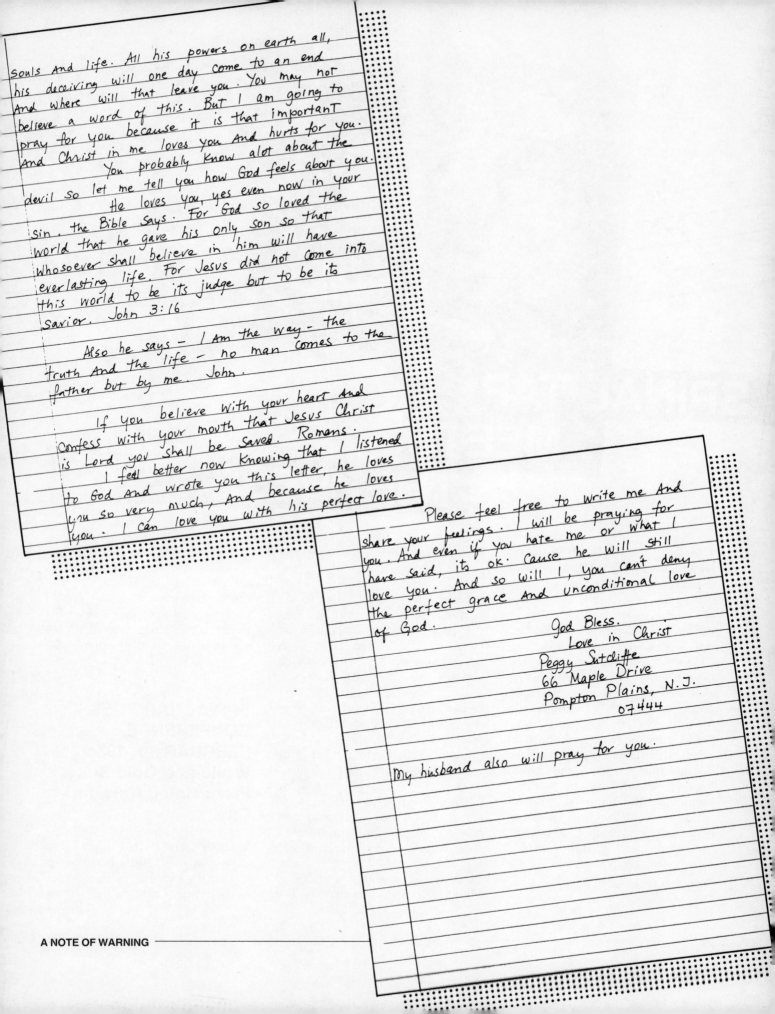

(Photo by Laurie Paladino)

SPINAL TAP MEETS THE PRESS

Platinum Returns

The White and Gold Suite of New York's elegant Plaza Hotel is actually more a kind of elaborate railroad flat than a suite per se: two narrow oblong rooms linked end-to-end and facing north onto Central Park, just a floor above street level. Named for its color scheme (white walls and ceiling with gold molding and trim), it was a fitting locale for a press conference and party held by Polymer records both to celebrate the opening of a new documentary about the band, *This Is Spinal Tap,* and to commemorate the band's LP, *Intravenus de Milo,* having been returned platinum.* (Perhaps the White and *Platinum* Suite

*Indicates returns of at least one million copies.

would have been more appropriate then.)

It was New York's chance to say "Thank you!" to Spinal Tap, and Polymer's chance to finally do right by them. The New York press came out in force, braving the icy weather and the even icier canapés, which clearly could not have emanated from the Plaza's legendary kitchens. A few pesky hecklers in the crowd, obviously forgetting that this was a press conference and not a rock concert, nearly marred the occasion with their thoughtless cries of "Louder!" But saner heads prevailed and the evening soon turned into a lovely affair.

The cast of characters included Marty DiBergi, director of the

"rockumentary," and several executives of Polymer Records, although tour manager Ian Faith, Polymer publicist Bobbi Flekman, and company chief Sir Denis Eton-Hogg were inconspicuous by their absence.

SPINAL TAP PRESS CONFERENCE, FEBRUARY 1, 1984 White and Gold Suite, Plaza Hotel, New York City

MARTY DiBERGI: I don't know if you know it, but I had the opportunity, I was given the chance of directing a film called *The At-*

tack of the Full-Figured Gals, and I turned it down. And I also turned down the chance to work with Sandy Duncan on a series of Wheat Thins commercials in order to make this film. I'm very proud of my association with Spinal Tap, and thereby an opportunity to get to know them as individuals and not just as a band. And I'd like to introduce them, three of the members of Spinal Tap: two lead singers and lead guitars, David St. Hubbins and Nigel Tufnel, and bass player Derek Smalls.

[They come onstage to applause.]

DEREK [shouting]: Rock 'n' roll!!!

NIGEL: Thank you very much, thank you!

DAVID: We'd like to thank, first of all, Mr. DiBergi, I mean I think he's definitely one of the primary filmmakers working in the field of *cinéma verité.* And this man really gives you a true twenty-four frames per second, but it's really louder than the last twenty-four, you know.

MARTY: Thank you, thank you, David. Thank you.

DAVID: We'd also like to take this [inaudible; loud feedback]. That sounds *so* good to me. . . . We're very proud to be associated with Polymer Records and, of course, the outfit they got to distribute them over here, Polygram. I'd like to say that we've been with eight—

VOICE IN CROWD: Louder!

DAVID: We've been with eight or nine—

VOICE: Louder!! LOUDER!!

DAVID: Louder?

DEREK: We'll do it louder LATER!

DAVID: I'd just like to say we've been with eight or nine record companies in our career . . . and Polymer/Polygram is number one! [Cheers]

DEREK: Actually it's number eleven.

DAVID: We want to thank you all for being here. You've been very kind to us. . . . We've never really achieved what we wanted to over the years in the States. But we're hoping that maybe we'll push it over the top now, maybe—

VOICE IN CROWD: You were a workingman's band, you were a working-class band.

DAVID: Hello?

NIGEL: I'd just like to say that, y'know, back in Squatney many years ago, y'know, we never thought we'd, uh, we never thought we'd be standing here together like this, y'know, and now we are. We're really proud of each other, and, uh, so this is for Squatney. All right, all right!

DAVID: Squatney doesn't really exist anymore; they tore it down to build a new club. So thank you very much. If you'd like to ask any questions, uh, go right ahead.

DEREK: It's great to see ya New York! [Applause]

MARTY: I'd like to introduce Russ Regan, senior vice-president, Pop Division, Polymer Records, who's going to make a historic presentation.

VOICES IN CROWD: Louder! LOUDER!!

RUSS: Three years ago, Polymer Records was proud—

VOICE: LOUDER!!!

RUSS: —proud as punch to ship this album gold. And I'm happy to announce tonight that we've taken it back platinum. [Laughter] Tonight, Spinal Tap has set record-business history. This is the first album presented to a group for one million returns. [Applause] That's the inscription here—this is their wonderful album *Intravenus de Milo:* "Presented to Spinal Tap to commemorate returns of more than one million copies of their Polymer long-playing record album *Intravenus de Milo.*" We're very proud to do this, and I'd like to add that we drew straws today and I lost, so I had to make this presentation.

VOICE IN CROWD: Show us the record!

RUSS: All right, guys, here you go. [Applause]

DAVID: Thanks very much, it's a great honor, and I understand it *is* unique, and we appreciate that.

VOICE IN CROWD: Louder.

DAVID: You know, the trouble is, we'd like to get louder but every time we get louder it feeds back because of the way it's positioned.

VOICE: Louder!

DAVID: Louder?

VOICES: LOUDER!!

DAVID: Get the guitars, they've asked for it!

RUSS: There are some other people from Polymer Records who were going to be here tonight but couldn't make it! Tonight Artie Fufkin is doing an in-store, and Bobbi Flekman is working on album covers for Deutsche Grammophon.... Ian Faith is in China working on the new Tap tours China tour. And Sir Denis Eton-Hogg is home alone; but he asked to come in his place the new president of Polymer/Polygram Records, Sir Guenter Hensler. [Applause]

DEREK: Quiet! Quiet, it's the president, please!

DAVID: There's a European speaking, quiet!

GUENTER: As you know, I've been a fan of yours for a long time; I've always found your music really confusable with just *any* band. Since Poly*mer* Records is actually becoming part of Poly*dor* Records, which again is part of Poly*gram* Records, I can really tell you honestly that [unintelligible]... But it better be good, because if it isn't, we just won't pick up the option, right?

DEREK: I want to say that's a refreshing dose of honesty in this business.

NIGEL: So we all know what's what then, right?

DAVID: What he's saying is this is a sort of pressure situation, is that it?

RUSS: OK, now . . . Got a really exciting announcement tonight. . . .

VOICE: What!?

DAVID: He says this should be exciting!

RUSS: Spinal Tap, in support of their new Polymer album, *Spinal Tap* [holds up cover, it is black]—and that's what it's really gonna look like on the market—

DEREK: Show 'em the back! [Applause]

RUSS: —and in support of their forthcoming rockumentary, *This Is Spinal Tap*, are going to be embarking on a major thirty-city tour—Spinal Tap's "Tap Into America Supertour '84." [Wild cheering] To commemorate this historic tour, for everyone that's here we're going to have a Supertour T-shirt as you leave [shows T-shirt]. Not only is this tour going to hit major markets, like New York, Dallas, and Atlanta, but it's going to hit heavy-duty metal markets like Valparaiso, Indiana; Hampton Roads, Virginia; and Bozeman, Montana.

VOICE: Rockin' Bozeman, all right Bozeman!!

VOICE: What about Philly?

DAVID: It's only a college town.

RUSS: And now I'd like to introduce to you the executive vice-president of marketing and distribution for Embassy Pictures, David Weitzner.

DEREK: He's good!

DAVID W.: We're really happy to announce tonight the opening of the rockumentary *This Is Spinal Tap:* New York, March second; Los Angeles, March ninth; Dallas, Houston, Toronto, the rest of the country all during March and April. Let's hear it for the film! Heyyy!!!! [Applause]

DAVID ST. HUBBINS: You all

remember David from his Atlantic Speedway commercials.

NIGEL: We'd like to open this up for questions right now. If anybody's got questions for us or Mr. DiBergi, you can ask 'em now, all right?

QUESTION: What artists influenced you?

VOICE IN CROWD: Louder!!

DAVID: The question, What artists influenced you? Well . . . well, I think my major influence is the black blues singer Blind Bubba Cheeks. He wasn't actually blind, though, he was not legally blind. He was myopic.

QUESTION: Is it true that after two decades of playing rock 'n' roll, you guys have severe hearing problems?

DEREK, NIGEL & DAVID: What?

DAVID: Next question.

QUESTION: What do you do when you're not playing rock 'n' roll?

NIGEL: [Inaudible]

DAVID: Any more questions?

QUESTION: You guys started in the 1960s, now looking back—

NIGEL: We didn't start in the nineteenth century, that's daft!

QUESTION: Nineteen *sixties*, the 1960s. Now looking back on all the change, do you think that rock 'n' roll has lost its importance as a social force?

DEREK: That's a really great question.

(Photo by Laurie Paladino)

DAVID: I think that in earlier times, rock 'n' roll was a music that represented something that meant something and was an important part of our lives. And nowadays, what it represents is something that's an important part of the music industry. I think it's changed in that way.

QUESTION: What do you call your haircut?

DAVID: Arthur, I guess. Is that the right name? We saw *that* movie in the U.K.

QUESTION: How do you feel about never having been nominated for a Grammy?

DAVID: Well, that's just a sore point with us, really, y'know, because in the U.K. we watch them on the hookup. You know, we don't feel that we've been well represented at the Grammys, I think mainly because there is no category "Best Foreign Song." I think if they'd just do that, we'd have a great crack at it, particularly with "Sex Farm."

DEREK: It's only fair, because the Oscars have "Best Foreign Film," so it only seems right.

QUESTION: What do you think of all the Spinal Tap bootleg records that are floating around?

DAVID: Well, we've sort of actually done those ourselves.

QUESTION: Will you be doing "Stonehenge" on the tour?

DAVID: Ah, yes, thank you. We'll be doing a scaled-down version of "Stonehenge."

QUESTION: Do you think your career was hurt when you referred to Don Ho as "a blind, ignorant Hawaiian"?

DAVID: I for one am amazed anyone overheard that that night. Any more questions? Questions? No? Well, thank you, New York!!

DEREK & NIGEL: Thank you very much!

PUBLICIST: Thank you for coming, and the group will be there to sign pictures and take pictures in the far room of the suite right after this, if you'd like to have your picture taken with them.

TAP ON WHEELS

During their stay in New York, Tap stopped by the legendary CBGB, where they were greeted backstage by longtime fan Gary Glitter. (Photo by Laurie Paladino.)

Following their historic press conference at the Plaza, Spinal Tap completed a busy round of promotional activities with a photo session by prominent New York photographer Libby Levenson and a return trip by limo to their hotel in fashionable midtown Manhattan. I had the immense good fortune to accompany Tap on both legs of the trip and to sit with them as they waited for Levenson to set up her lights and seamless. What follows is a running interchange with Nigel Tufnel, David St. Hubbins, and Derek Smalls, joined by current Tap drummer Ric Shrimpton (Mick's brother). Intended originally for publication in a teen magazine for which I was reporting at the

time, the interview never saw the light of day. It appears now for the first time, in its entirety. Not one word has been cut.

—Ed.

INTERVIEWER: *Do you have any sympathy for the German heavy metal band Scorpions who have had their latest LP rejected by some American stores for being too sexy?*

NIGEL: Too sex*ist*.

No, theirs was too sexy.

NIGEL: Well, there's a difference. I was told in the film that I went to see that was made about us, there was a thing where they said that. I think it was a mistake, actually. I don't think there's a difference really between sensual, visual, and occupational.

But they deserve everything they get that band [Scorpions]. I mean they're rip-offs right from the word go.

DAVID: I mean, they're bleedin' Krauts, innit? You can't be German. . . . British heavy metal by Krauts? Come on.

NIGEL: No, you can't be, by the rule of thumb musically, German and do anything—except fix a bloody sausage or a glass of beer.

DAVID: Or build a car.

NIGEL: Yes; make me a fast car, gimme a glass of beer, fix my clock, and go away. But don't play rock 'n' roll, and don't play it that loud. Please. That would be my request. I mean on my tombstone that would be my request.

But they were the first people to recognize the Beatles.

NIGEL: They didn't recognize 'em. They allowed 'em to do a couple of gigs. Big deal. This whole German thing's a bit overdone, innit?

Do you see yourself at the age of forty still playing "Hell Hole"?

NIGEL: If I can remember the words, yes is my answer.

[Derek Smalls enters, and joins the conversation.]

I was just asking Nigel here if you guys see yourselves at forty still playing "Hell Hole."

DEREK: I *am* forty! But I don't look in the mirror, so I don't see myself doin' it.

You look young for your age.

NIGEL: Well, you got people who say, y'know, I get six hours sleep or whatever. But it's not the amount of hours you get per night; it's the amount of hours you get in your whole lifetime. Then it's divided by the age that you are. So people who say something like, Well, I slept for two hours last night—it don't matter. 'Cause last month I slept all day one day. That made up for it. That's the whole trick to staying youthful.

RIC SHRIMPTON: As long as it averages out to about eight hours a day.

NIGEL: It's maths, all I'm saying. It's maths.

RIC: He keeps a little chart....

In your film, Spinal Tap never really discuss their sex lives much....

NIGEL: We did—they cut it out of the film.

Can you tell us now, do you guys have steady girlfriends?

DEREK: I do. I've got the steadiest.

NIGEL: Yeah, she's steadily going downhill.

DAVID: He's so jealous. He can't, like, really develop a serious relationship.

Why is that?

DAVID: I don't know, I think he's weak.

DEREK: He's only weak the morning after.

NIGEL: I find that having a lot of women really keeps your bloodstream going. I go after quantity.

DEREK: Rather than quality.

DAVID: Believe me.

NIGEL: Well no, they've got to be under twenty-two, that's my only rule; and not in a hospital bed, that's my only rule.

DEREK: Under twenty-two at a time is what he means.

RIC: Anything between six and sixty in a skirt is more like it.

DAVID: His rule is anything that casts a shadow.

NIGEL: Casts a shadow with tits . . .

DEREK: Anything not recently killed.

Can you remember your first crush?

NIGEL: My first what?

DAVID: *Orange* crush!

NIGEL: Oh, that one, yes. No, no, no, I used to like, uh, barley . . . what do you call that? Barleycorn?

Derek and David sandwich MTV veejay Nina Blackwood while fellow veejay Alan Hunter buddies up to Nigel after press conference at the Plaza.

(Photo by Laurie Paladino.)

I meant a romantic crush.

NIGEL: Oh, *that* crush. I thought you meant . . . Yeah, I remember. I was going to school in Squatney. And on the way home from school, where my mum sent me, I saw this little girl across the street, little tiny little birdie. And I, uh, I took out my, uh, y'know, what you call in America, my, uh, *wanger.*

We can't print stuff like that in a family publication.

DEREK: Call it a ding-dong then.

NIGEL: You can say that I dropped my ding-dong.

RIC: Dropped his ding-dong.

DEREK: Showed her a bit of the old Sweet William, didn't you?

NIGEL: Yeah, I did.

DAVID: Roger the Dodger.

NIGEL: The little chap with the fire hat came to visit . . . and she was amused.

At this point, Libby's assistant entered and led the boys in for makeup. I discreetly turned off my tape recorder and waited. An hour and a half later, we were in a limo, speeding (well, creeping) from Levenson's Chelsea studio to East Fifty-fourth Street and the band's hotel room. Once again I turned on my reliable Sony TCM-111 and recommenced to record history.

So how's the tour going, guys?

RIC: Tour? The world tour was canceled.

DAVID: The citywide tour is doing very well. We're going up-

town, downtown, and that's it. Taking the world one neighborhood at a time.

What do your parents think of all this?

DAVID: My dad is, uh, passed away.

NIGEL: I haven't told my folks yet.

What are you waiting for?

DAVID: His dad doesn't read the papers, y'know.

NIGEL: He thinks I'm working at a mill in Yankford. That's up in the north, up near Yorkshire.

DAVID: It's near Wankford.

DEREK: My dad's real proud, real proud. I used to go round with him in his little truck every week—

In a lorry, you mean.

DEREK: Van. He has a van that he goes about to people's houses in and he sanitizes their telephones once a week. People worry about the germs, y'know. It's true. So he sprays the receivers.

I didn't know that.

DAVID: Well, since the plague in the, y'know, twenties, I suppose —no, it was before that—the early part of this century—

NIGEL: The black one.

DAVID: —and there's still a racial memory of this terrible influenza fad that—

NIGEL: No, that doesn't mean it was a racial thing, actually; they

called it the black plague because—

RIC: It was a rac*ist* thing, not racial—

DAVID: No, a racial *memory* is what I'm saying, and people who are not old enough to recall when it was—

DEREK: Are condemned to repeat it.

I read somewhere that Eddie Van Halen has an amp that goes up to eleven now.

DAVID: No, he craves one, he wants one. He got the idea from us.

NIGEL: Someone he knew saw the film, and he wanted to know where we got the equipment.

DEREK: Is there any air conditioning in here?

How many hotels have you been thrown out of?

DAVID: For nonpayment? Not a lot.

No, for disruption, the usual mucking about.

NIGEL: We don't trash 'em as much as we used to.

DAVID: There was one hotel where the management came up to the room and *asked* us to trash the room—

DEREK: For publicity.

DAVID: —for publicity purposes. They'd heard that there was a band staying there and there was no damage done to the hotel. They were not booking the big groups anymore. So they asked us, as representative

The Men of Tap.

Derek struts his frets an hour upon the stage.

Blissfully ignorant of stateside scam, the real Spinal Tap find time to pose with a couple of London's finest, neither of whom is named Rita. (Photo by Karen Murphy.)

Nigel takes off in Japan.

David in a characteristically blissed-out moment. (Photo by Steve Meltzer.)

Ric Shrimpton in action. (Photo by H. Shearer.)

Tap is sometimes criticized for copycat antics, but the original choreography of Derek and Nigel is nothing to sniff at.

Playing to bigger crowds hasn't numbed Derek's thumping drive on this tour. (Photo by Steve Meltzer.)

Two faces of evil!

(Photo by Steve Meltzer.)

(Photo by Steve Meltzer.)

(Collection of the author.)

Pre-Omega Point Tap: Viv Savage, Mick Shrimpton, and Derek Smalls at play in happier times.

English rockers with not a lot of reputation at stake, to go ahead and do the job for 'em. But we couldn't do, couldn't really bring ourselves to do it—

RIC: He was pleadin'. He was on his fuckin' knees.

DAVID: —unless the mood struck us.

NIGEL: They make things a lot stronger. I took one of my old Strats and I bashed it against the telly. Didn't even break.

The television didn't break?

NIGEL: No, nothing broke. So where does *that* leave you?

DEREK: Nowhere.

DAVID: It's a disappointing, frustrating feeling.

NIGEL: Tried tearing the curtains, nothing worked.

DAVID: But there was one time—

DEREK: Tried burning them, but they wouldn't even catch fire, they just smoked.

DAVID: There was that one time that we—

NIGEL: So I just took my pillows and I stuck 'em in the tub, got 'em all wet. That will show 'em.

DAVID: There was one time we drained the oil or something out of the tour bus and put it in the swimming pool and set it alight. Remember that? It was a *mo*tel; it was in, oh, Alabama or someplace.

DEREK: But then we couldn't move the bus.

DAVID: We couldn't make our getaway, no. But it looked great, it looked great.

DEREK: It was a good five seconds—and then a bad two hours. Yeah, watching those chaise lounges [sic] melt up into little balls alongside of the fire—

DEREK: A couple of the old ladies, too, as I recall—

DAVID: Yes! Well, they were already 'alfway there, weren't they?

NIGEL: They went into little balls when they saw us for the first time.

RIC: They're into any kind of balls they can lay their hands on. *Bawlls!*

DEREK [pointing out of limo window]: Oh, look, I'll bet you can go in there and they'll tell you a great old story: the New York Yarn Center.

DAVID: You'll hear a new yarn every day. Old pop will tell you tales of the woods.

We were talking about girlfriends before, and you didn't all answer as to whether you had steady girls.

DEREK: Well, I've been through a very unpleasant divorce.

DAVID: Yeah, he's off women, this one. So to speak.

NIGEL: Never was *on* 'em.

DEREK: *In* 'em but not *of* 'em.

RIC: In the *flesh*, he's off women.

DAVID: Off quickly, too.

NIGEL: On and off.

What do you think of this guy Boy George—do you think he has a future?

DAVID: A future as a small sofa, I think.

DEREK: An occasional piece.

NIGEL: A sectional.

DAVID: Look, a lot of rock 'n' roll has counted upon the outré, the bizarre—

DEREK: The what?

DAVID: The outre.

DEREK: What tray is that?

DAVID: No, you can go a bit over the top sometimes, y'know, and I think he's at least over the top, don't you?

DEREK: And back down to the bottom again.

NIGEL: For the first five minutes it's amusing to wear clothes that women wear. I mean, we've been through that.

RIC: David did it.

NIGEL: Well, he did it for personal, dating reasons. . . .

DAVID: I had one period of my life when I dabbled in an alternative life-style, *merely* to explore the commercial possibilities—

DEREK: That's not what you said then—

DAVID: —during the Bowie, the glamor days . . . no, no, it was the glitter days, the glam days, y'know, and I did give it a try, I gave it a whirl. . . .

RIC: We all gave it a bit of a whirl.

DEREK: Read his interviews at the time—he seemed *very* committed to it.

DAVID: I wound up tied up in the alley behind the hotel—

NIGEL: And that was the end of it.

DAVID: —and that was the end of it. I said, "Fuck this...."

DEREK: Well *that* was the start of it.

DAVID [shouting]: I said, "Fuck this, I'm going back to *pants*."

NIGEL: He said, "Lubricate this first, *then* fuck it."

RIC: I actually think that dresses for men is *almost* a viable thing, but we just have to wait a few more years for men to actually embrace the idea.

DAVID [pointing at Nigel]: *He* wears a kilt. He wears a bloody kilt.

NIGEL: Come on, come on, that's historical.

DAVID: It's hysterical.

NIGEL: It goes way back, way back on me mum's side, it goes back to her grandparents, who came from Aberdeen. And, you know, Dundee or someplace.

DAVID: You don't even *know*?

NIGEL: Oooh, y'know, I haven't seen the tree in years.

DAVID: His dad was a Jeopardy.

RIC: A Geordie, right?

NIGEL: No, he was from Yorkshire. He moved to Scotland.

DAVID: Oh, that's where he got the kilts from?

It's so hard to keep track of these British districts.

RIC: You've got to understand, it's a small country, but the people are sort of like . . .

DEREK: Tribes.

RIC: Yeah, tribal, it's a very tribal, ancient, uh, thing.

NIGEL: Really, no, the people that live, let's say, in Yorkshire won't speak to someone who comes from Tunbridge Wells.

DAVID: No, they won't. They *can't!* They can't understand each other.

DAVID: The teeth are—

DEREK: In the wrong place.

DAVID: —a different shape, and the tongue, it's all like *dialects*, like. It's all very inbred.

RIC: Yeah, Dr. Who and the Dialects.

DAVID: Oh, stop! Dr. Who and the Dialects.

Does that account for the fact that so many different musical styles can come out of such a tiny, otherwise insignificant country?

NIGEL: Wait a minute. Let's not start putting down a country that—Well, it's not insignificant.

I only meant insignificant in terms of—

DEREK: Size.

NIGEL: Then why isn't India running the world, eh?

It's a former British colony, what do you expect?

DAVID: Thirty years ago the only rock 'n' roll produced in *this* country came from a small handful of black people, y'know? Hardly representative of the Eisenhower era, as I understand it. So it's not like—you've got to look at the oddball, y'know, and perhaps the British Isles has more than its share of odd balls.

DEREK: When half the men are homosexuals to begin with, and the other half are fucking their sisters, what do you ex*pect* you're gonna get?

DAVID: No, he's bitter that the British divorce laws have cleaned him out . . . and he's bitter that he doesn't have a sister! But I do think the British are a very special race. I think a fucking comet or something passed over the U.K. in the early part of this millennium—

RIC: Dropped some medieval fairy dust—

DAVID: Some sort of thing happened to us, and we invented rock 'n' roll and acting. All in one gulp, y'know?

And they called it Heavy Metal.

DAVID: Yes. Sort of a hybrid, innit?

I also hear that you fellows are considering moving to America to avoid the British tax laws. True?

DAVID: He [Nigel] bought a castle in Scotland—he got bad advice.

NIGEL: I didn't get the right advice from my solicitor, because he said that if I bought a castle—

but he meant in Lichtenstein or someplace like that—that I could get a tax break. . . .

DAVID: If he had become a United States citizen, *then* he could've bought the castle and saved a whole passel of money; but he didn't do it that way. This way, he's paying all of Maggie's salary, and a bit more.

Whatever happened to your girl-friend, David? Jeanine?

DAVID: She didn't come over this trip.

Is she still running the band?

DAVID: No, she's just running *my* life. You know, that's the way I like it.

DEREK: She's running it with one big thumb.

DAVID: We had a bit of a group session. I understand their point of view, the other members of the band. . . . I have decided just to shave her off the fuzzy part of our career.

DEREK: She's running his life and it's a hands-on experience.

DAVID: Yes, exactly; I understand how that could be a problem.

NIGEL: Ginny's very user-friendly.

DAVID: And I do, I am, of course, they do not understand, the two of them . . . there is a way, y'know. . . . Perhaps not a great businesswoman, but a great *woman* woman, if you know what I mean. . . . And that's something they can never know, except sporadically. When she has a few too many.

DEREK: In brief spurts, as it were.

OK, let's see. We talked about Black Sabbath stealing your Stonehenge idea for their shows.

ALL: Yeah . . .

We talked about Scorpions—

DAVID: Well *they*'re Krauts—

—and their awful album-cover experience. . . .

RIC: It's not awful, we sympathize with them, you know, we do.

NIGEL: Happens every day, donnit?

RIC: Except they stole it from us.

NIGEL: You know that whole Beatles record with *Sergeant Pepper*—

DAVID: How about the white album—burned *me* up.

NIGEL: Yeah, but *Sergeant Pepper,* that whole thing where they wanted to, y'know, make 'em do another cover . . .

Wasn't that Yesterday . . . and Today?

NIGEL: With a bunch of babies, butcher babies, yeah. . . .

I think you've got the wrong cover.

DEREK: Look, there's Hitchcock!

DAVID & NIGEL: Nah, he's dead.

DEREK: A Hitchcock lookalike in our film would've been great. He's now taking bit parts in his own death.

DAVID: What's that place, is that Toots Shor's or is it "21"?

NIGEL: Either way, you gotta wear a necktie to go in *there.*

DEREK: Even the women.

DAVID: No, if you walked in in silks, if you walked in in jockey silks I bet—

NIGEL [pointing to jockey statues in front of "21"]: That's why those guys got shrunken, because they tried it.

RIC: They're all holding on to a ring, too. Is that significant?

DAVID: That's from the Tolkien books—those are the Lords of the Rings there.

DEREK: The Jocks of the Rings.

I think that's so they can chain them up at night so no one walks off with them—like the galley slaves.

DEREK: Galleria slaves.

NIGEL: They used to steal those galley slaves—take 'em in the middle of the night if they weren't chained down, it's true.

DAVID: Shrink them.

DEREK: Look, *there's* Pastrami 'n' Things.

NIGEL: So, is this the end of the interview?

I guess so, unless you've got anything else to say.

DEREK: Shut the machine off, then.

NIGEL: No, we'd just like to say that—no, nothing.

THE WORLD OF SPINAL TAP

Like many of you out there, I am an inveterate collector. My bookshelves and closets and desk drawers, even my kitchen table-top, overflow with piles of this or that collectible—from simple stamps and coins to matchbooks from around the world to the inevitable display cases of ceramic thimbles imprinted with the logos of forgotten food products of a younger, happier America. And then there is my agglomeration of rock 'n' roll memorabilia: buttons, posters, backstage passes, and, of course, *stacks* of rock magazines, fanzines, tour books, and the like.

It is from the latter collection of priceless artifacts of the past and near-past that I have assembled the next portion of this book. It ranges from the earliest fan's-eye views of Spinal Tap in America to news reports on a bizarre impersonation scheme, to full-length features in more recent rock publications on the band's background, personal facts and figures, intimate reminiscences, even tips on equipment and playing techniques. My sincere hope is that you the reader will find as much fascination and enlightenment in perusing these articles as I did from snipping them out in the first place.

Come with me then as we journey ever more deeply "inside" the very private world of Spinal Tap—a world of witches and warlocks, demons and demiurges, and strange, mystery places in the heart of the rock 'n' roll dreamscape . . . but also a very real world where perfectly ordinary, everyday things can and do happen. Let us begin.

One of the first American press conferences, with 2nd Tap drummer Eric "Stumpy Joe" Childs, c. 1969. (Photographer unknown.)

GIRLS WHO GOT TO MEET THE BOYS

These are the lucky teenagers who managed to make contact with Spinal Tap. Here are their personal reports.

Sheryl Nelski, Age 17
Yorktown H.S., Yorktown, Ind.

I had won grand prize in a WYND Spinal Tap Poster Contest and we were attending the Tapsters' Indianapolis press conference. The questions went something like this:

Q: What do you do with all your money?

DAVID: Mostly, I let Sarah handle the monetary affairs. She's very good at starting small businesses and nearly making a profit.

Q: When you do a new song, how do you decide who sings the lead?

DEREK: It's a matter of range, really. Nigel has a sort of lowish soft thing going, while David tends to get louder, higher. And *faster*. I can do the screams.

Q: How do you sleep at night with your hair that long?

NIGEL: Eight hours isn't that long to sleep with my hair.

Q: Why wasn't Spinal Tap included on the program at Woodstock? Didn't they invite you guys, or what?

DEREK: They did, but we were busy at the time.

NIGEL: That's been raised a million times, that question. And

the answer is, I think it was lost in the mails. I think they *did* invite us, and I think we just didn't get the letter.

Q: How did you feel about that at the time?

NIGEL: Well, at the time, y'know, not getting the invitation and then only hearing about it a month after the Festival itself, it was all right, y'know?

DAVID: Woodstock?

During the questions they were all kidding and joking among themselves. They were all smoking. David, who was chewing gum while smoking, was carefully scanning the crowded room.

The questions ended and all of a sudden I heard the disc jockey who was our host say something about a dedication. He came rushing over to us and told us to grab our poster. Then tripping over wires, cameras, and cameramen we made it up to Tap.

All I remember is the disc jockey introducing us and saying something about our poster. David and Derek were nodding at it. Then, minutes later I was holding Nigel's hand and just looking at him. He asked if something was wrong, but I just couldn't utter a sound. He smiled and they were quickly ushered out of the room.

We then ran upstairs to listen to them perform, but left a few minutes before they were finished. We pushed past a guard who blocked an entrance to the basement—that must have been where I received multiple runs in my stockings although at the time I didn't have any memory of this happening—and ran to the gate. It was covered by a tarpaulin which we pushed back just in time to see a laundry truck pull away. Its contents—Spinal Tap bound for their hotel.

—Sheryl Nelski

Taken from *Datenight*, October 1969

Teens Interview Stars: Spinal Tap (Formerly Thamesmen)

By Lita Motiff, Age 16
St. Joseph Academy,
Green Bay, Wisc.

GREEN BAY, WISCONSIN: Plans were made with me and seven others to be at the Holiday Inn, room 226, at 11:00 P.M. Object: an interview with Spinal Tap. I had to leave the show before everyone else to get to the hotel in time, although why, I don't know, since Spinal Tap obviously didn't leave until the show was over themselves. But maybe they had a fast driver, or maybe it was the limousine.

My sister-in-law drove me and my friend Randa to the inn at a speed I didn't think anyone was capable of. It never struck me that Spinal Tap could ever make it before us, so I was prepared to wait for them to appear. I said to my friend, "I wonder how long it will be before they get here," but before I had the words out of my mouth, David (they had arrived with a police escort) came up to me, said hello, introduced himself, and asked if I would like his autograph. I said, "Of course," and then we talked about all sorts of ordinary and wild things.

They were so nice, you can't imagine how they make you feel. Like they're your best friends and you've known them for years. David has a great ability to love all people and to carry on a conversation with ease without even knowing you. He is one of the happiest people alive, and you can tell this by the way he acts and talks.

I gave Derek a ring I'd had for several years and had worn.

"What's this for?" he asked.

"To wear," I answered.

"OK," he said, and put it on his little finger. Then he said wait a minute, that meant we're engaged. This seemed to worry him, and he took it off and gave it back. Altogether, he wore it about thirty seconds. (The next night, when they were on stage again, I caught Nigel's eye and threw the ring to him, but I couldn't tell if he got it.)

It was really more like a party. We just sat or stood around and talked with everyone there, about school, cars, our interests, etc. David asked if anyone would like a Coke; he even said that if we wanted to we could take off our shoes.

Here are some of the things we talked about and discussed, all in a very small nutshell:

Q: David, did you ever have any singing experience or lessons?

DAVID: I took a sort of lesson once from our minister. I was having trouble reading the dots in our hymnbook and he gave me a bit of help after chapel, but just the once.

Q: Where do you get the ideas and inspiration for the songs you write?

DAVID: We use very few actual *ideas* per se in our songs. As for inspiration, the woods are bloody *full* of that.

NIGEL: They come as dreams. I wake up, usually about three or four in the morning, having had a dream, and that's the beginning of the song.

Q: Like, for instance?

NIGEL: Well, "Stonehenge" happened like that. I woke up, and I woke up knowing some of the words. I was sleeping with a young lady I had seen the night before—she was a Eurasian lass —and I woke up sort of suddenly and I just said, "Stonehenge, where the demons dwell, the banshees live, and they do live well.'' And I wrote it down—I keep a little notepad by my bed —and I got up and went over to my piano room and started working on it. Then I ring up David in the morning, he comes by, and we finish it off.

Q: Who writes the words, the music, and so forth?

NIGEL: What I usually do is I think of the initial theme, musically, and the first few lines. David finishes off the music and the words, and then usually I write the bridge. Y'know, it works out.

Q: What group to you think is the best in terms of talent and sound?

DAVID: Haven't heard the best yet. When I do, and after I've compared them with their peers, I'll let you all know.

Q: What do you think of protest songs?

NIGEL: Protest songs? Like, I don't want you anymore? That kind?

Q: No, I'm thinking more of the political sort.

NIGEL: Oh, political. Well, I'm really a firm believer in "Leave your politics in the voting booth, and if you wanna sing about it,

do it on your own time.'' I mean I *do* vote, and I do believe everyone should vote, but *don't* sing a song about it; don't do that to me, please.

DEREK: If you mean ''Eve of Destruction,'' that kind of thing, I don't know. That isn't the vibe that we want to send out. We want to send out a positive vibe, which is why we did ''Flower People.'' To me, a protest song is . . . How can you dance or rock or move your body or shake your fist or your fanny when you're going, "Oh, right, the politician's being bad''? That's "head" music —and I don't mean psychedelic —not rock 'n' roll. That's not what we're about. Rock 'n' roll is sex music, body music. Head music is like for Frank Sinatra. Frank Sinatra should be singin' protest songs, logically. When you figure it out, it makes sense.

Q: Gosh, I don't know. What kind of protest songs would *Frank Sinatra* sing?

DEREK: ''Get off the Backs of the Mafia, Bobby Kennedy,'' or whatever. But I mean, it makes sense. ''Let's Put Hoffa Together,'' y'know? I dunno what's on 'is mind, but somethin' like that.

Q: Are you political? Would you serve in the army?

DEREK: We don't have the draft in Britain, of course. If there were an attack on Britain, of course, I feel very strongly that it should be defended. I'm not one to get dressed up in a drab uniform and shine me boots twice a day and go off and kill Germans. I'm not sayin' it's wrong—it's just not what I was made to do. I might play in the army *band*, might play tuba or something, that's the bass of the army band. I don't *know* the tuba, but while the rest of the geezers are out killing Germans or Russians or whatever, I'll be practicing the tuba. And I'd put in a good, solid, honest day on the tuba for my country, I would do that. I think anybody who *wouldn't* do that at a time of danger to their country, y'know, should be shot for a traitor.

DAVID: Too young to get political—too old to serve. Next question!

Q: Why do you wear your hair so long?

NIGEL: *Why* do I, or *where?* Where . . . on top, obviously. Why? I don't even think about things like that. It just grows, doesn't it? The answer to that question is: It grows, doesn't it?

Q: Do any of you read music? David?

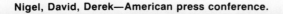

Nigel, David, Derek—American press conference.

DAVID: I can read hymnbooks.

DEREK: I read *about* music, which to me is more important. No, we're not schooled orchestra players or anything like that. Sir George Barbarolli is not gonna invite me to play in his next Promenades concert, no.

Q: Do you ever get taken for an American group?

DAVID: No. We were once *traded* for an American group.

Q: Where is Squatney, exactly?

DAVID: At sort of an obtuse angle to the right of the embankment and straight on till morning.

Q: How did you feel about the death of your drummer?

DAVID: Which one?

NIGEL: There were several, you see, who died. [Sighs] Well, you know, each bloke is a different bloke, and you feel differently about each one. The last one I didn't really, to be perfectly honest, I didn't really care about. But our first drummer, you know, Stumpy and all that . . . I mean, it hits you quite hard to have a member of your group that you've been creatively involved with, y'know, die. It's quite a traumatic thing. . . . But, it's also amusing. Sure. You've got to look at death on the light side once in a while, and think: Well, sure, he's dead, innit sad? But it's sort of funny, innit? That's the way I look at it.

Q: Derek, can you tell us about your cars?

DEREK: Let's see: a Lamborghini, Land Rover, Chevrolet Monza (just for Pamela to drive around in town). There was a '58 Cadillac convertible which was a lovely kind of a moose of a car; it was chartreuse, and then Pamela had it painted a multicolor. This was a little bit influenced by *The Fool*—you know, the guy who does those paintings for Apple; they repainted it with union jacks all over. So that's the stable.

Q: That's pretty impressive. . . .

DEREK: It is, but not compared to Nige. Nige, I think, is the car maniac of the group. He has quite a stable, innat right, Nige?

NIGEL: I don't like to talk about my cars, but, yes. In fact, I believe I have cars on three continents at the moment.

DEREK: Whereas mine are just basic entertainment.

Q: Boy, it must be hard to keep track of cars on that many continents.

DEREK: It's hard for him to keep track of that many *continents!* They mount up on you.

Q: I saw a picture of the three of you on a motorcycle, and it said that you were all wild over the sport. Are you really?

DEREK: "God made more off-road than road. So be it!"

Q: Nigel, during the riot on stage tonight, a girl slipped something into your boot. What was it?

NIGEL: Yeah, well, usually what happens is it's either a phone number or a ring. Lots of times they drop their rings in there. Then after the song I go upstage towards the amplifiers and take off my sneaker or boot and dump it out. One of our roadies keeps a Baggie backstage, and if it's a ring he usually keeps it and sells it—and if it's a phone number, I keep it. We've got a spotter, y'know?

Q: What's that?

NIGEL: It's a bloke who works for us. He stands onstage by the amplifiers where you can't see 'im, and he cases the house to see if there are any cute birds. And if there are, he gives 'em a backstage pass and they come and see me, don' 'ey? Call 'im a spotter. I mean, I don't have time while I'm playing to do that work myself, obviously.

Q: David, what did you feel last night when the fans mobbed the stage?

DAVID: I generally despise that sort of thing, but this one geezer actually repaired my phase-shifter on stage last night, so you never know.

Q: What do you think of your fans?

NIGEL: [Yawns] Well, they're the greatest fans in the world.

DAVID: They are tomorrow's warriors on the battlefield of rock!

Q: What do you think of teenagers who smoke pot or take drugs of any kind? What would you say to them?

DAVID: The money you're spending on that garbage goes up in smoke (or whatever), but a great record album is forever.

NIGEL: Well, *my* word of warning is to really take it light. Because it ends up that you really have to start thinking about where your life is going. It just doesn't pay in the long run, it really starts to eat into you. So if you can go light, that's my advice, go very light.

Q: What does that have to do with drugs, exactly?

NIGEL: Oh, I'm sorry. Well, I don't approve, then. That's my answer, I don't approve.

Q: You've never used drugs yourself then?

NIGEL: I didn't say *that*. I said: Don't approve.

Q: What about alcohol, booze?

NIGEL: Don't approve.

Q: But you do drink sometimes?

NIGEL: Well, you know, we're not talking about me. You asked about the kids, and I don't approve.

Q: Are you saying there should be a different standard?

NIGEL: No. It's a different *question*, though.

Q: Why did Ronnie Pudding leave the band, and do you feel any animosity towards him?

NIGEL: *Oh,* yeah. There was quite a bit of animosity, actually—*huge* animosity. I'd say *screaming hatred* was more to the point.

Q: What caused that?

NIGEL: Theft of material, you know, sexual innuendo . . .

Q: Towards whom?

NIGEL: Towards anyone he could be within five feet of. He was quite an amoral bloke.

DAVID: Actually, I dunno about that, Nige. Y'see, Ronnie was very close with a chick singer named Lhasa Apso who worked with us—you remember, Nige?

NIGEL: [Makes barking noises]

DAVID: Right, well, when she got the boot, it gave old Ron a heart blister. Carried it around for a year—then split when "Flower People" hit. Tried it solo, disappeared.

Q: But he *wrote* "Flower People." Didn't you feel—

NIGEL: No.

Q: Do you want to offer an opinion of his album, *I Am More Music?*

NIGEL: Nope. Never heard it.

Q: Do you listen to other musicians much?

NIGEL: Yeah, but probably not ones you've heard of. . . . Little Elliott was my first real . . . I still listen to him. James Brophy, Irish rock 'n' roller, has a band north of Dublin a little bit. Great. I like Jimmy Alfano, great blues player, from Maine.

Q: Derek, were you at all intimidated by the prospect of having to fill Ronnie Pudding's shoes after he left and you were hired to play bass?

DEREK: No, why? I would've been if he had done any of the writing and it was "OK, mate, where's the next hit?" But all he'd done was the one song, so . . . I did have to simplify his bass parts a bit—he was a bit fussy, a bit precious in his parts, y'know. So I just boiled 'em down to their essentials so that the meat part came through and the froufrou, the salad, was left for the "art" bands to do. 'Cause we're not an art band, and I think that was Ronnie's problem.

In fact, it was quite thrilling to be a part of something I didn't have to be in on the long, slow climb for. Quite a change from Skaface at Brighton, playing for the holiday-makers with bellies below the knees going, "What's *this* music?" Bournemouth was the worst for that kind of scene. So from there straight to Number One International Hit, no, I didn't feel intimidated. I felt, At last, Derek Smalls, you have arrived where you belong. Sometimes I would chant that to myself.

Q: Onstage?

DEREK: Depends how high I was. "At last . . . Derek Smalls . . . you have arrived . . . where you belong." You can see the rhythm of it.

Q: Do you think you'll always be famous?

DAVID: No. But *we'll* always remember us.

NIGEL: Don't know. And it's not that important to me.

Q: What *is* important to you, Nigel?

NIGEL: Uh, the gold standard. . . . No, don't write that. What's important to me is that the world as we know it learns to live as one, and that they make a capo that doesn't break.

Taken from *Teen-o-rama*, August 1970

Appearing on the American summer-replacement television series "Jamboreebop," Tap perform their hit song "(Listen to the) Flower People."

My Beautiful Experience with Spinal Tap

**Yolanda Pavanne, Age 16
Cooper H.S.,
Minneapolis, Minn.**

Suddenly flashbulbs began to pop and the air immediately became beautiful. For Spinal Tap were making their way into the room.

I stood inches away from the front row. One man in front of me must have realized the anguish in my heart for he put his arm around my waist and pushed me in front of him. I patted his shoulder and said, "Oh, thank you, I just luv you!" He smiled, although the cramped space forced him to be wedged uncomfortably against me from behind. No matter.

Derek was in front of me, as was David. Next to Derek was beautiful Nigel Tufnel, the last to sit down. I forgot all about the camera in my hand; I just sat staring at them for a few moments.

I'd collected a gift for each Spinal, never thinking I'd really ever get the chance to give them to them. David looked down at me and I said: "Best wishes to you and Sarah." (I'd

dreamed about saying that so I had to say it.) He smiled and said, "Thank you." His voice was deep.

Next, Derek. I yelled to him, "Derek I think your wife is beautiful!" His face beamed with pride and he said back with a grin, "Thank you."

The boy I love more than anyone in this world sat an arm's reach away from me and I didn't know what to say. Finally I took an envelope holding a huge souvenir cigar from under my arm and handed it up to Nigel. I said, "Here, Nigel, this is for you." He opened one corner of the blue envelope after reading the writing on the front that said, "To Nigel, Love, Yolanda." He smiled sweetly when he read that. He pulled out the huge cigar, his mouth dropped, Derek looked at it and said in a low husky voice, "Oh, a cigar!" All four kept saying over and over "Oh, a cigar!"

I was so proud! Nigel put the cigar in his mouth and immediately photographers went crazy, for here was a center of attention. Everyone began yelling at Nigel, "Hold up the cigar, Nigel, put it in your mouth!"

He did exactly what the cameramen wanted. I wanted to appear sophisticated as possible and not just some other screamy Tap fanatic (which I am!) but at one moment I could not help but show all the pride I had for Nigel holding my (his) cigar. My lips were pressed hard together and my eyes on the verge of closing in ecstasy. Nigel looked down at me! I straightened up right away, but I knew he saw how very good I felt.

I asked Derek if I could shake his hand. He looked at me blankly, then extended his hand to me. Talk about a heart stopping!

I'd written a poem and short letter to David. I took it from under my arm, got David's attention easily for he was close, then said, "Here, David, this is for you." He took the paper from my hand and quickly put it in his pocket, then looked defiantly at anyone who might question what it was. (I think he thought it was some mushy love letter or something.)

Knowing that Derek was a champion Monopoly player, I had brought a small red hotel along with me. I reached up to Derek: "This is for you." He looked at my hand then asked after a long pause, "What is it?" I said, "I know you're a Monopoly player and I thought you might like this." For a minute I didn't think he was going to take it, but finally he bent over and took the small item from my hand, stared at it, while David broke his neck to see what it was. David yelled, "Oh! A hotel, ho." Then as the other Spinal Taps had done before they all chanted in, "Oh, a hotel!"

After a few moments Nigel bent across the table and said about his cigar, "I don't smoke these, ya know?"

I asked David if I could shake his hand. All the microphones and equipment were in our way. Somehow I moved my hand above all the stuff and reached David's hand, but not before my hand collided with a small microphone. I knocked it over. Derek made a face, then straightened up the microphone and said, "Hey, we don't want to knock down all this equipment here!" David coldly stared at Derek, then hit him in the shoulder, saying jokingly, "That's no way to talk to the girl, Derek!" Derek, with his usual sad-eyed expression, looked at me, then David, then down to the table. He was so cute, I felt sorry for him, even though David was only goofing around.

Derek was chewing gum and blowing huge bubbles throughout the entire conference. But whenever a cameraman would ask Derek to blow a bubble for a picture, Derek would always shake his head and say, "We're not allowed to!" Nigel has the most sarcastic expression on his face at all times, but this makes him all the more strongly handsome.

Shaking hands with Nigel posed a problem. He stood above Derek and I asked if he'd shake my hand. He looked at me as if someone had painted my face green or something. He put his hand out finally, then seemed to change his mind, then put it up again and shook my hand. He sure is a weird, but funny, man! He scared me because I thought maybe he wasn't going to shake my hand.

Whenever anything goes on, David is always looking to see exactly what is happening. Nigel is very sweet, considerate, good-looking, and single! I love him. Derek is very funny and is always saying funny things. He smoked more than the others and seemed to find pleasure in blowing smoke rings. Also David has the creamiest skin in the world, he's thin but not exceedingly so. He's really tuff!

All these things happened within 7 minutes.

I sauntered back to my front row seat and began telling this one girl what happened to me while I was up front. She seemed interested in something else so I just made a face at her and sat down.

—Yolanda Pavanne

Taken from *Teen Scope*, November 1968

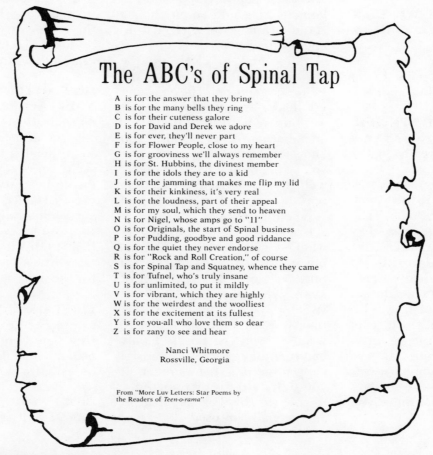

The ABC's of Spinal Tap

A is for the answer that they bring
B is for the many bells they ring
C is for their cuteness galore
D is for David and Derek we adore
E is for ever, they'll never part
F is for Flower People, close to my heart
G is for grooviness we'll always remember
H is for St. Hubbins, the divinest member
I is for the idols they are to a kid
J is for the jamming that makes me flip my lid
K is for their kinkiness, it's very real
L is for the loudness, part of their appeal
M is for my soul, which they send to heaven
N is for Nigel, whose amps go to "11"
O is for Originals, the start of Spinal business
P is for Pudding, goodbye and good riddance
Q is for the quiet they never endorse
R is for "Rock and Roll Creation," of course
S is for Spinal Tap and Squatney, whence they came
T is for Tufnel, who's truly insane
U is for unlimited, to put it mildly
V is for vibrant, which they are highly
W is for the weirdest and the woolliest
X is for the excitement at its fullest
Y is for you-all who love them so dear
Z is for zany to see and hear

Nanci Whitmore
Rossville, Georgia

From "More Luv Letters: Star Poems by the Readers of *Teen-o-rama*"

NIGEL TUFNEL

NAME: Well, my name's Nigel Tufnel, innit?

MOST MUSICIANS WE TALK TO HAVE MIDDLE NAMES. Yeah, well, I don't.

BORN: Squatney, London. It's in the East End. I was born in 1948.

WE NEED A MORE SPECIFIC DATE. You do, do you? Cor, I hate doing this, I really loathe it. . . . March first.

SCHOOLS: I went to the same school as David, y'know. The name's been changed, as they say, to protect the innocent. We used to call it Fidget-with-Me school, because basically that's all these old geezers would do. You'd arrive at school in your little shorts and your little cap, and they'd try to get a little knuckle up your bum. It was quite rude. Saint Scubbage was the first one we went to. You don't say "Saint" over there, you say S'n' Scubbage.

AND WHO WAS SAINT SCUBBAGE? That's David's department, you'll have to ask him about it.

JOBS: We had to chip in a bit at home, so I would do anything I could around the city just to make a few bob. Used to get a farthing just to clean up the chewing gum in front of the Bakerloo Station. They haven't got farthings anymore, they left 'em out. What it used to be was one-quarter of a penny. You know, you've heard of one penny, you've heard of a ha'penny bit— well, this was even worse than that, this was a farthing. Just to scrape the gum up.

I also had a job working at what we call Marks and Sparks, but it's really called Marks and Spencer, sort of a department store. When you'd get seconds, sweaters and things like that that weren't perfect, I had to write "2" on the boxes. I only had that job for a week, 'cause I kept forgetting the number. If you write a three or something, it goes to another department and gets all confused.

In Battersea Amusement Park there's this slide where you sit on sort of like a doormat and you go down this little spiral sort of slide on this sort of horsehair mat. And my job was to comb them out at the end of the day. 'Cause all these fat, smelly kids had been sittin' on 'em, and I'd take a wire brush—got about three quid a week. It was grotesque, I had to wear a nose pin, especially in the summer.

HOW OFTEN DO YOU WASH YOUR HAIR? Well, it really depends. If we're touring, I try to wash it every other day, 'cause we're playing every night. If I'm seein' a bird regularly, she makes me do it pretty much every day, even if she has to throw me in a shower herself. But I don't like that squeaky-clean puffed-up look. I think it looks a little poufta, a little wimpy; so I like to go for the more greasy sort of look.

FIRST BAND YOU WERE IN: I s'pose The Lovely Lads was the first time I got to really flex my own musical muscle. It was sort of a scuffle band.

DON'T YOU MEAN SKIFFLE BAND? Well, skiffle was so snotty, y'know, so we called it scuffle. And once in a while we'd bash a few heads, yeah..

ANY REMINISCENCES OF RONNIE PUDDING? Very inventive sort of chap, y'know—he'd write music! He knew how to make those little dots, he'd make these little sort of balloon things on this lined paper and everything, and link 'em together with little strings and all that, the whole bit.

He played an interesting bass, also; he played a half-fretless bass. The first three or four frets had frets, and then it was fretless from then up.

WASN'T THAT CONFUSING? Well, not to me—I wasn't playing it. It was his problem, really, and he dealt with it quite well. It also kept people from borrowing his bass.

LAST BOOK READ: Well, I'm still reading it; OK? I'm trying to get through this *Book of Lists*, and it's so fucking confusing, because you can't remember anything. I'm about a quarter of the way through and I have to go back all the time. I can't really progress farther than that 'cause it seems I can't remember what is listed where. It's been close to a year, but that's the last book officially. Before that, I tried to read *The Book of Kells*.

ISN'T THAT REALLY OLD? Oh, yeah—I mean, it's a reprint, it's not the original. That's in Ireland somewhere; but I couldn't get through this either, it's all these pictures. But I like mysteries, generally.

WAS THAT A MYSTERY BOOK? Well, it was to me; I don't know if it was meant to be. I like the *idea* of reading mysteries. I can't really

get through most of them. But I like the idea of saying that I read mysteries, so you can put that down.

FIRST GIRLFRIEND: Her name was Diane Curtis. I met her in a milk bar in the West End. She was down at art school, a very beautiful woman, and we, uh, thrashed about a bit. But then she met a bobby; he had a regular job so she went off with him.

FAVORITE DRINK: Glenlivet right now is pretty much all I can drink. Previously, I used to like ginger beer. That was my first love, and then when I started needing something with a little more kick to it, I went to Glenlivet.

FAVORITE DURAN DURAN RECORD: I've never heard one. I've heard of the name, but I've never seen or heard them play.

WHAT TV SHOW DO YOU ALWAYS TURN OFF? I don't have a television, so you can say All, I suppose. I stayed at a rented cottage here in the States once where they did have one, and I couldn't figure this little box out. You hit these buttons, but it was mostly writing on the screen.

THAT WAS CABLE TV. Yeah, well, it keeps changing, and I can't really see the point of having a *book* on television. So I'm not really that familiar with television.

My only real memory is Sooty —he was one of my favorites. He was a puppet and he had a little magic wand.

PETS: I've got a bird—not a girl, a parrot. It's called a conure, from South America.

HOBBIES: Not really, because my work is my hobby. You could say collecting guitars, I s'pose, or you could say my interest in English history as it pertains to heavy metal music. "Stonehenge" and all that is really my doing—it comes from my interest and research into the legends of British lore; that's sort of my department in the group.

WHAT OTHER BRITISH LORE DO YOU HAVE UP YOUR SLEEVE? The Arches at Wimpdon, which are these old Viking ruins that no one knows the origin of but I'm thinking of maybe going up there and maybe trying to write a suite based on them.

WHAT WAS THE WORST PERIOD OF YOUR CAREER? Well, it's pretty consistently bad, y'know. I think right after I did *Clam Caravan*, my solo record, was maybe the very worst.

IT DIDN'T SELL TOO WELL, DID IT? It didn't sell at all. I think according to BMI, it sold none. And you know, you've got to worry about that, 'cause you think you've got some friends or family that would've gone down to a record shop and bought the record. Sold *none*. So I was quite depressed for about six months after that.

WHO WOULD YOU LIKE TO BE STUCK IN A LIFT WITH? Male or female? Anyone I'd like? ...I think, um, Willie Shoemaker. He's so small, he'd give you a lot more air to breathe, wouldn't he? He's a jockey, you know.

MOST EMBARRASSING MOMENT: We did a show on the Isle of Skank, which is north of Aberdeen or someplace like that;

anyway, my strings broke, *all* the strings broke—I think it was sabotage—on the first number. That was the most . . .

DIDN'T YOU HAVE A SPARE GUITAR THERE? No, that's what was so embarrassing.

MOST TREASURED POSSESSION: A hanky my dad gave me—just a plain old white hanky. I keep it with me at all times in my guitar case; it's just sort of sentimental.

YOU DON'T ACTUALLY BLOW YOUR NOSE IN IT THEN? No, I wouldn't dare.

WHAT WOULD YOU SAY TO MARGARET THATCHER IF YOU COULD? I think I'd just look at her. I feel I've said everything to her that I've got to. In person, you mean? Oh. I'd say, y'know, uh, How's it hangin'? That's what I'd say.

COULD YOU DESCRIBE YOUR BATHROOM? I've got three. In Scotland I've got my large residence, I call it—I don't like to call it a castle, because people get sort of put off—and I've got three W.C.'s, as we call it. One is for any girls that might come by. It's got a bidet in it; it's got a large sort of sauna tub–like thing, sort of Jacuzzi thing; it's got Spanish tile on the floor and a red ceiling, which I always like to have, a red ceiling in all my rooms—it just keeps the blood going a bit if you look up. If you ever noticed, when you put your head back, the blood goes out of it, so you need to be reminded to not do that, and that's what reminds me.

My personal bathroom is just a very masculine sort of thing. I've got a lot of car magazines and I've got a scale and an old grandfather clock; and everything is black in my bathroom—black toilet, black sink with brass knobs.

FAVORITE VIDEO GAME: I like the one with the little, um, uh, what do they call those things? No, I don't, I don't like those things; I can't figure them out.

SO WHAT DO YOU DO TO RELAX? I play. I play my music, play my mandolin or play my guitar or have a bird over and she kisses me. One of my favorite things, y'know, you say, "Hey, uh, 'dya like to come over and, uh, go around the world a bit? And then they come over and kiss you on the neck. I like that.

AROUND THE WORLD? That's a euphemism.

WHEN DID YOU LAST SPEAK TO YOUR MOTHER? Me mum calls me every Sunday, she calls me collect. If I'm on tour, I call her, every Sunday.

LAST RECORD BOUGHT: I bought a tap-dance-instruction record. I just like the sound of it. I tried briefly to give it a whack, but it's too fucking complicated, innit? Especially on record, you can't see what they're doing. I mean, they've got these little pictures inside but I can't figure it. I just listen to it in my car—I made a cassette; I like the sound of it.

STRANGEST GIFT FROM A FAN: I got a four-course Italian dinner under foil, and I couldn't quite figure if it was loaded with drugs or what they were doing, but it was just a bowl of spaghetti with meatballs, some steamed zucchini, and garlic bread. Under foil. It was hot, too.

WHAT DO YOU WEAR TO BED? I don't wear anything at all: nothing. I have a very large king-size, extra-king, whatever they call that, and I have these very imported Italian sheets, and I don't wear anything.

SORT OF AU NATUREL, EH? You got it, mate.

WHAT DO YOU DO ON A RAINY DAY? Well, I stay in, I guess. I don't have a TV, so that settles that thing. Again, I'm really quite a big fan of having the young ladies over whenever possible, and on a rainy day, of course, you lounge about, listen to the music, play a bit, frolic in it.

DO YOU HAVE A LOT OF GIRLFRIENDS? I do, yeah, I got to admit.

NO STEADY GIRL, THEN? No, you'd like to think there would be at my age, I suppose. I'm looking . . . I'm always looking for the one that will be *the* one—Mrs. Tufnel. As a matter of fact we had a contest once: "Could You Be Mrs. Tufnel?" There were a lot of nice entries—if you'll pardon the expression—but it didn't really amount to much.

If you've got any ideas, you could have people write to me, y'know, care of the fan club. Have them send photos in, though; I need a photo.

FAVORITE APPLIANCE: Electrical or, uh . . . ? That's an interesting question, it's quite interesting. . . . Uh, I like those little sponges, those little round sponges that you can moisten postage stamps with. That's my favorite. They sit in a little glass dish. . . . I'm quite intrigued with those.

WHAT EXACTLY ABOUT THEM? I don't know, I think it's the natural beauty, I guess, of them.

DO YOU BELIEVE IN ASTROLOGY? Not in the classic way. I believe it has some hand in what happens, but I don't strictly believe in it, no. I mean, I'm sure that some of it means something, but some of it doesn't—that's the way I look at it.

HOW DO YOU RESPOND WHEN PEOPLE ASK WHAT SIGN YOU ARE? I don't tell 'em the truth, first of all. Like I told you I was born March first—I wasn't. I like to throw 'em off a bit. You can even put a question mark after that, because y'like to keep 'em guessing about that stuff.

DID YOU LIKE *GREMLINS*? I didn't see it.

WHAT WAS THE LAST MOVIE YOU DID SEE? The last movie I saw was on an airplane. I saw this thing where this woman came out and said that if there was turbulence or something, loss of cabin pressure, these little things fall down with these little hoses attached—I liked that quite a bit.

BUT THEY DO THAT ON ALL THE FLIGHTS, IT'S JUST A SAFETY DEMONSTRATION. I MEANT A MOVIE, A FEATURE-LENGTH—Oh, a real long one, you mean? A long movie?

ON A SCREEN, YES. Oh, I see. Uhh, 'cause I like that rather, quite a bit, actually.

YOU MUST GET TIRED OF THAT ONE. Well, no, I kind of like it, 'cause I know it's so predictable. It feels comforting to

know what happens in the middle, beginning, and the end and all that. I like to *know*. . . . Aside from that, the last movie that I saw was *The Lone Ranger*.

DID YOU LIKE IT? No.

PERSONAL MOTTO: It's a Latin phrase: *Otium cum Dignitatum.* It means Leisure with Dignity. That's the official Tufnel coat of arms.

WERE YOU EVER A HIPPIE? No.

WERE YOU EVER A PUNK? No.

WHAT KEEPS YOU AWAKE AT NIGHT WORRYING? I have sort of a recurring nightmare that I'll go out on stage and someone's retuned my guitar to open tuning or something, and I'll start to play and it's just not even close. That *wakes* me up. And then what *keeps* me up is, uh, I don't like high humidity at night 'cause my legs stick together. So what I do is if there's a bird stayin' over, she takes a big tin of talcum powder and she just lines my inner leg with a really, y'know, large portion of it, and it slides about a bit more and then I can go back to sleep.

IT MUST GET ALL OVER THE SHEETS, THOUGH. Well, that's all right, innit?

YOU HAVE THOSE BIRDS TO CLEAN 'EM FOR YOU, HUH? You got it.

FIRST RECORD BOUGHT: "Say You Do" by Little Elliott.

FIRST CONCERT: It was a little club. I went to see the Arab Boys, I s'pose.

FAVORITE URIAH HEEP RECORD: Nope. Never heard one.

HOW HAS YOUR LIFE CHANGED SINCE THE SPINAL TAP MOVIE CAME OUT? Well, there's a lot more interest, or attention, I would say. It's sort of a mixed blessing, I s'pose, to be portrayed in, uh, sort of the light that we were. Not entirely positive. You've seen it, right? It's sort of a half-baked impression of the tour, wa'n't it? It was clearly not that ragged, y'know.

IT DID TEND TO SHOW THE DOWN SIDE OF THINGS. Well, sure, that's all Hollywood for you—Show 'em the underside, don't show 'em the glory.

DID YOU WATCH THE OLYMPICS? I saw a little bit—not at home, being televisionless, but in a pub I saw a bit of it. I saw the people shootin' a rifle, which was not very interesting—but you know what I find about that, I think that's a trick. Because you can't see the bullet, right? So who's to say that there's not some bloke in back of the target, you know, with a ballpoint pen or something just shovin' it through?

BUT IT'S THE OLYMPICS. . . . Well, sure, yeah, but y'know, I'm just saying, "Prove it to me." You can't, so that's sort of lost its luster for me. And I saw these people running over these, um, boards—what do they call that? Well, they're sort of boards in the middle of the track.

HURDLES? That's it, yeah; I like that a bit. I don't understand why they put them there, but it seems as though it would sort of just break up the rhythm of the running a bit, but I like that one. And I saw some of the swimming, but I'm not really into that stuff too much, to be honest.

DO YOU PREFER CURLING? Well, I don't like curling either; I do like cricket and I like football —English football, of course. My team is Manchester United, that's the team I follow. I'm a booster of the Manchester United team.

FAVORITE MONKEES RECORD: Never heard one. Nope.

DO YOU BREAK? No, I don't.

HOW DO YOU FEEL ABOUT BREAKDANCING? I don't know, I think if you're eleven years old, if you're black, it's one of the few things you *can* do, so do it. I mean that in terms of opportunity, if you can make a few dollars out of it, then do it. Leave me alone, basically.

HAVE YOU ANY O-LEVELS? Oh, no, I didn't even get close to that, no. That's for the upper-class sort of kids, the educated people. I mean I didn't even, not even close.

WHAT HAVE YOU GOT IN YOUR POCKETS? That's rather rude, innit? Y'know, I mean, here we are, we're doin' an interview and there's a bloke at the other end, he says, "What have you got in your pockets?" I mean that sounds like, if you want to ask me out to dinner then you do it, but you don't say "What 'ave you got in your pockets?" I mean, that's rather rude. . . .

WELL, WE'VE GOT A LOT OF YOUNG FEMALE READERS, NIGEL; I'M SORT OF ASKING FOR THEM. Oh, *I* see; well, make yourself clear, then. Don't, y'know—I didn't know if the interview was over and you were askin' me or what. . . . Uh, well, the left side of my trousers is of course taken up by, uh, y'know, the Pink Oboe, as we say, or One-Eyed Willie. That's pretty much crowded-in there, you can't really get much in that side pocket.

The right pocket, uh, just one sec . . . I've got some American money, I've got the one with the big nose, he looks like he's wearin' a wig or something—a quarter-dollar, it says—and I've got a plectrum, flat-pick you call it, always carry a flat-pick with me. And I've got a phone number, hmmmmm. A crumpled piece of paper with a phone number on it, and her name is Terry. And I don't remember where I got this or why, but I'll give it a ring after I talk to you. There's a little heart written on it, so maybe that means a little "month in the country" action, I don't know.

Normally I don't carry a wallet of any kind; my road manager usually keeps all the money so I . . . don't have a credit card, can't get one. Back pockets, once in a while I carry what I call a "detangler," a comb. I don't like to comb my hair, but if it gets sweaty in the summer, I like to get some of the nubs out. I like to scratch my head with it actually, more than even comb, get the little bugs out. And that's about it, really.

In the old days I used to carry what they call a "torpedo umbrella," but those days are over with, aren't they?

A TORPEDO UMBRELLA? Yeah, well, a condom.

BRITISH SLANG IS SO COLORFUL. Oh, thank you. That's not even British, that's just pure Squatney. But I don't do that anymore; what with these pills that these women take, it's really not even required.

LAST FOWL DECAPITATED: I don't even know what that means.

THERE IS A GUY IN THE MUSIC WORLD FAMOUS FOR BITING THE HEADS OFF BIRDS. I know what you're talking about—I'm just playing dumb, I don't really want to comment on that. Just say, "No comment." If you look back to the question as to what pet I have, you'll see it's quite repugnant.

Taken from *Mega Hits*, June 1980

DAVID ST. HUBBINS

NAME: David Ivor (as in Ivor the Engine-Driver) St. Hubbins. Ivor's me dad's name. It's really not all that unusual; it's not a very popular American name, but it's used quite often in Britain. It's one of those that did not really survive the Atlantic crossing. Ian's done quite well; Colin's beginning to catch on and all that; but Ivor's gonna stay behind.

BORN: August 13, 19wuhwuh—I would say 1943, you might as well just say it out. I was born in Squatney, England, in the Squatney Women's Hospital—me mum was a woman, at the time. Squatney's in sort of the southeast corner of the Northeast End.

SCHOOLS: I went to the Sulfur Hill Academy for Boys. It was,

like, the only really nice public school me mum could afford, mum and dad. Dad didn't make too much money, you know. He repaired luggage—he had a traveling stand and he used to go to tourist areas. He'd travel around the beaches a great deal during the summer when people were there on holiday, 'cause everyone was always breakin' the handles off their luggage and all this and he was like the Johnny-on-the-spot. And that's what it said, in fact: Johnny on the Spot. For years I used to think that his name was Johnny, even though me mum called him Ivor, or else she called him dad. Actually we *all* called him dad. . . .

IS ALL THIS TALK OF CORPORAL PUNISHMENT IN BRITISH PUBLIC SCHOOLS EXAGGERATED? Well, it certainly was exaggerated in ours, I

must say. It was incredibly exaggerated. It was grotesque. I can't compare it to anyone else, but I think that maybe we had a rougher breed—a rougher breed of gentility. We were sort of like upwardly mobile types, but we knew we didn't belong in the public school system, so there was a bit of hell raised. But I was more of an instigator myself. I never really went in for any real cruelty, but I loved eggin' others on to perform it.

JOBS: I never really had one. I'd do odd jobs, and I'd do a bit of moving or re-moving, as we call it, but I always managed just by busking on the streets or selling songs—we were always able to sell a few songs. And we could scrape by as musicians, even if what we were doing was not reaching any sort of great fame or anything.

WHO DID YOU SELL YOUR SONGS TO? Groups, local groups. Blue World China; they didn't release anything over here, I guess. Blue World China actually had a few sort of skiffle hits, jug-band stuff, and in the early days we actually sold 'em a few songs.

HOW OFTEN DO YOU WASH YOUR HAIR? It depends. I just take a quick look at the shape of it, and if it looks like a map of Greenland or something, you do something about it, you give it a wash. Otherwise, I'm not vain, y'know. I'm not vain until there's someone there to be vain *with*. Jeanine, my woman, really serves that purpose for me. She is my reflection and she tells me, "You look like shit," or whatever, and I go and do something about it.

LAST BOOK READ: Strange, I just finished it a few hours ago. It's about communicating with spores, forms of, like, prenatal plant life, and how certain spores and molds and smuts—you know what smuts are—how they, because of their very minute size, might be actually more in touch with existence as a definable source than we will ever be. In other words, they're not thinking creatures, but they are somehow, if we could communicate with this nonthought that we would have. . . . It was just a marvelous book. I sort of skimmed through the end because it got a bit technical, but it seemed to make a pretty good case. It's by Lowell Curtin.

FIRST GIRLFRIEND: She was from Germany, and she was the daughter of the housekeeper of this friend of mine. She was the first real, sensational, all-involving crush I ever had—her name was Diana. Her dad was Spanish or something and she was a great-looking girl. I don't know what happened to her, I was only with her for about six months and then she had to go back home because her dad got deported; but she was the first one I was really *gone* on. When you have a really heavy girl

friend early on, you start comparing all others to her, and it was not until much later in my life that I was ever actually able to relate to other women.

FAVORITE DRINK: It's called a "smoothie." It's a lot of fruit and bananas and protein if you like in a blender; but then you put a piece of semisweet chocolate in there and let the blades batter it up a bit, so it's like a chocolate-chip thing. You don't dissolve the chocolate, you've got to do it just right.

I don't drink alcohol unless I'm with other people. In other words, I do drink from time to time, but I don't think I have a problem anymore. There were times in my life when I really couldn't handle it, but I think that since I found my sea legs personally, I don't really need it as much anymore. So I try to stay healthy instead.

FAVORITE DURAN DURAN RECORD: I don't know the name of it, but it's the one where he wears that billowy shirt. I didn't really listen to the music part, but that shirt was great. What do you suppose they do with their shirts once they, y'know, go to a new style, because they do change their—oh, never mind, I think I know their manager.

WHAT TV SHOW DO YOU ALWAYS TURN OFF? I'm a bit obsessive about TV, especially when I'm in the States. Over in the U.K. I'm not really much on it, but there's some great European TV. There was a Finnish program I caught one time when we were on tour—it was all about torture in the Third Reich. It was *films* of torture in the Third Reich. I had to turn that one off—I just thought it was a right *downer*, I suppose you

could say. I'll always turn that one off; if that comes on again, I'll always turn that one off. If that becomes a series, for example, I'll try to be out of the house, with the TV tuned to another station.

You know what I turned off in the States, though? I was up real late one night in Austin, Texas, 1982, and there was this station that—what it did, it had this little mechanical camera and it panned sort of a board. . . . It had a clock, told you what time it was, and a barometer to show you what the pressure was, and a *thermo*meter that told you what the temperature was, and they panned it back and forth so you'd know all these things. I watched that for about half an hour and I couldn't make any more of that, so I'll always turn that one off, too.

PETS: Jeanine has two Shar-Peis: Mr. Pip and Dragon Princess—we call her Dragon. I call her Drag, to tell you the truth! No, I love 'em, I do. Strange-lookin' dog. You know what it looks like? It looks like it was a larger dog with tighter skin, and then someone grabbed him by the anus and pulled him as hard as he could, and the face has sort of collapsed inward. And that's the best I can describe it. I think they're hideous. They've been with us for about two years now, and still I'll wake up and see them in the morning and I scream. But I love them.

HOBBIES: I guess you'd call sort of like general self-improvement my hobby—you know, learning more, knowing more. I do have sort of a new fascination: I've begun to learn about my blood. I've got this kit where you test your blood chemistry for various things—and it's like findin' out twenty-four hours ahead of time that you're gonna be sick to death the next day. It's great. That's become like a hobby. People come over the house and I take a little blood from their fingers, make a smear, and I tell 'em, y'know, "You got smooth sailing for another bit." 'Cause you can really tell, you can really get to spot these little buggers, find out that there's a deficiency in whatnot and, you know, you're gonna be constipated next weekend—it's great. I know I haven't got the brainpower to be a full doctor or anything, but I love to learn about me own blood.

WHAT WAS THE WORST PERIOD OF YOUR CAREER? There was a time when the band sort of split apart a bit—this is not the time that you see suggested in this film, this documentary they made—*that* wasn't anything at all. This time was a time when legal matters kept us from recording at all or playing under our name. We did a few benefits and whatnot under false names—the Cadburys, we called ourselves at one time, I recall . . . Anthem . . . of course, there's now a group called Anthem, isn't there?

Most of the time, Nigel was in his castle in Scotland, and I was bouncin' about a bit—at that time I was actually spendin' some time at home with me mum; me dad had just died—and we were being prevented from recording by our old label, Megaphone. They got an injunction against us ever setting foot on any professional stage or recording-studio floor. So if we could've found a way to hang from the ceiling and work, we would've done that.

WHO WOULD YOU LIKE TO BE STUCK IN A LIFT WITH? I think that bloke who was on "All Creatures Great and Small." I've always wanted to ask him, y'know, if he really puts his hand all the way up the cow's bum, like he does on TV. Bloke reaches right up there, you know? It's not just a three-knuckle job, he's all the way up to his biceps. I've always wanted to ask him that. Of course, it wouldn't take long—the lift would have to get going again fairly quickly after I got me answer to that one, I s'pose, but . . . I'm so curious about that one.

WORST JOB YOU EVER HAD: Gee, I'll tell you the most unpleasant job I ever had; it's not like a real filthy job or anything, it's when I was an apprentice locksmith when I was a kid. There was like two—I guess you got to call 'em what they are—these two huge lesbians who were havin' some sort of quarrel. One had locked herself into the bathroom and proceeded to get herself chained up to the grille of the window, and it was just a—well, it was more of—it wasn't such a bad job actually, now that I think about it. It was rather amusing; I sort of looked forward to the—no, skip that. I like working, I really do. Let me think about that one a bit more. Maybe I'll come back to it.

MOST EMBARRASSING MOMENT: I can't use any names, but there's a famous black rock 'n' roll star of the Sixties and early Seventies—I won't mention his name because it wouldn't be right. I ran into him in a hotel lobby and I called him by the name of another, extremely well-known late-Sixties early-Seventies black entertainer, who I also can't name. And it was very embarrassing, because the

subtext there is always, Does he think that I think they all look alike or something? And it couldn't be further from the truth—I mean, these two did look quite a bit alike, but otherwise . . . I felt bad about that. He never said anything about the incident; in fact, he died shortly after that, and I sent flowers to the family of the other one, but it's not worth going into.

MOST TREASURED POSSESSION: It's a sixteenth-century Celtic harp. With the name Harry Lauder carved in it. Harry Lauder was a very famous Scottish entertainer. I've had it assessed, and the harp itself is worth quite a bit, but the signature's a forgery. I couldn't part with it for the world; it's a beautiful piece and it's just something very special to me, although I've never actually played it in public. I've fooled with it a bit and I've done some private recording with it, but it's such an intricate instrument and you can't bend the strings like you can with a guitar, so it's purely a showpiece. What it basically is is a forged Harry Lauder harp, though I don't even understand why. You can't *cash* a harp, I don't think.

WHAT WOULD YOU SAY TO MARGARET THATCHER? I don't really like to get too much involved in politics, but to Margaret Thatcher I'd like to say: Let the bloke speak a bit more. This is reverse sexism to not let your husband say anything, and I think he's such an intelligent-looking bloke, we'd like to hear more from him. So it's basically, Get off his back, just let 'im have 'is day a bit, let 'im out a bit.

Do you know Mr. Thatcher over here?

DIDN'T EVEN KNOW SHE WAS MARRIED. Denis Thatcher, he's a *remarkable* person, he just reeks remarkableness. I've just seen him on telly, y'know, sitting next to her and, like, standing behind her and smiling. You can tell he'd be interesting if he had a voice—he's wonderful.

DESCRIBE YOUR BATHROOM: Well, how 'bout this? I'm staying in this place in southern California—it's really beginning to grow on me after three months, so I'll describe the spa area. It's done like Japanese-style, sort of like a deep red wood; it looks a bit like someone took a great lot of patio furniture, bolted it together, and made this thing. And it's got this great circular hole in the middle and then bloody-hot water in it—I mean, it's *really* hot water.

So, you get in and you sit there and you just kind of take it all in. It's like a huge flat doughnut you're sitting in the middle of. You look up and there's these eucalyptus trees lolling over you in the warm breeze, and these jacarandas—I'm learning the names of all these flowers—and blue sky and some power lines, and a Graham Chapman bird. You know Graham Chapman from Monty Python? He does this bird [imitates squawk]. And otherwise I'm just layin' here, I'm about to fall asleep. But it's great, 'cause I don't sleep in New York, I don't sleep in London, I don't sleep in the seaside in the U.K., I don't sleep in Europe— but I sleep like a *baby* here.

HOW DO YOU RELAX? I come to southern California! I do. And I also stare at one color, something that's one color, like a sock. It's like reading when you're not quite sleepy enough, and I like to read sometimes, but when I really want to relax I stare at one color and it usually works. Because, y'know, there's so little tussle if you're only concentrating on one sight, one color.

FAVORITE VIDEO GAME: There's this one called Breakdance—Breakdance something, Breakdance Breakdown or something like that. And it's like you get these five little black people and they do breakdance, they do headspins and all this stuff, there's a certain skill level to be able to do. And you've got to watch out for these manholes. You've got to have someone else from your breakdancing team, you've got to get him to moonwalk over and put the lid on the manhole before you do your headspin across it, because you fall in, you die and then there's only four of you, you know? It's great, it just came out.

WHEN DID YOU LAST SPEAK TO YOUR MOTHER? On her birthday, I guess, which was in June sometime. She's fine, she's staying with a friend she's known since they were teenagers, who lives in Birnham-on-Crouch, which is in England on the east shore. She generally lives in Squatney with her sister, another widow.

IS SHE SUPPORTIVE OF YOUR CAREER? No, I make my own living now; she doesn't have to support me at all. . . . Oh, I see what you mean. Oh, yes, of course. Because she always wanted me to be more than just a tradesman. She respected me dad a lot, but if he could've come burst into the spotlight with a pair of Spandex pants on and be grossly overpaid for it, she would've been just as happy. But, failing that, she thinks it's fine that I do so.

LAST RECORD BOUGHT: It's called *Hooked on Missa Luba*. It's a Congolese mixed children's choir doing Missa Luba, which is the Congolese Catholic mass. It's a fairly old record, but they've remixed it and they've added, like, a really sharp disco beat, and a lot of claps and stuff.

STRANGEST GIFT FROM A FAN: I got a microscopic slide of someone's skin one time. Someone peeled it off of some part of her body—I don't know really— and they made a permanent slide, cemented a little glass pane over it, and mailed it to me. I went around to a chemist's and had a look at it. She had taken such meticulous care with it, I half expected to see in the microscope "Hello, David" or some sort of intricate message. But nothing of that kind really occurred.

WHAT DO YOU WEAR TO BED? Green, mostly. I have a number of green items I wear to bed, nothing really fancy. I don't know why green—I've always slept in green. I think a lot of times I find myself staring at the sleeve of my pajamas, they're helping me fall asleep.

WHAT DO YOU DO ON A RAINY DAY? I like to go out and stand in the rain. I take a brush and comb sometimes, take a rinse. 'Cause I love standing in the rain, but people see you standing in the rain they go, "What's wrong with you? You're bloody daft." It's a problem of mine: I want to appear like a rational human being, so I take a brush and a comb and I give it a bit of a whack. It helps out.

HAIR CARE: Yeah, I stand out in the rain with a brush and a comb. "See above," I guess you might say.

FAVORITE APPLIANCE: Oh, I know what it is. I've never seen one, but it's a puffed-wheat gun. You know puffed wheat, the cereal? It's those guns that they're supposed to shoot them out of. I've always wanted to see one of those. It's not really my *favorite* appliance, I suppose, but it's the one I'm most curious about.

DO YOU BELIEVE IN ASTROLOGY? Yeah, I've got to say that I do. I don't really adhere to it as much as I used to—there was a time, I think, when the tempo, the pace of things, was a bit different, back in the late Sixties, I suppose, and we all had a bit more time for that. Since then, I've let a bit of it go, but I've got to say that I still want to know that about people because you never can tell. Did you *know* that they've figured out that everything in the universe interacts to some extent? So there's no reason why Saturn might not have some effect on you: It is a body in the universe; it has to interact with you in some way. So why not take some wild guesses and say that you'll, y'know, probably marry someone with blond hair? It's when they get specific it doesn't work, but it's fun.

YOU LIKE ASTROLOGY IN GENERAL, THEN? Yes, well, I like *all* that. I'm really fascinated by the way people have been able to discover these, like, orders out of supposed chaos. I've never been so good at it myself. I mean, I still stare at the sun and I say, "Why?" And then I say, "Ouch," because you know, I stared at the sun too long.

But some people really sit down with a pencil and paper and they say, "I know. We'll say this bunch of stars that looks like a lion—when the sun goes through there, then these people are gonna be grouchy, while *these* people are going to be fun-loving and creative. It's, like, they made a *stab* at order—I think it's admirable, y'know, even if it's, y'know, a complete, y'know .·.. fake. Better to stab out in the darkness than to light a single match.

DID YOU LIKE *INDIANA JONES AND THE TEMPLE OF DOOM*? No, I haven't got around to seeing either of those yet. You'll have to put me down for that I'm waitin' for the novelizations.

PERSONAL MOTTO: God, I've got so many. I hear things that people say, little bits of wisdom, and I try to hang on to them. 'Cause I'm not really much on thinking them up myself. But I did think of something the other day—in fact I wrote it down and I keep it in my wallet. I don't really know what it means or what made me think of it, it was just something I said in a radio interview: "A shallow genius is better than a deep fool." It's the only one I ever really came up with on my own.

But I had a friend who used to say something that impressed me quite a bit. His name was Coy Devin and he lived in the same building I did, which was right next door to where Nigel lived on the corner. Coy was a strange bloke. He was into munitions and stuff. He was a sort of terrorist later on, I s'pose, but—but at this time he was just a bit of an amateur hellraiser—no political ends. But he said—I never really understood it but I loved it —he said: "If you want to swing, you've got to hang." You know? Isn't that great? It's not really my personal motto, but it's one that I've always sort of liked.

WERE YOU EVER A HIPPIE? If a hippie, as I understand it, has to be poor, I never really was, because by the time they were called that, we were already beginning to make a few bob. So we weren't impoverished and we didn't have to go to visit the Diggers or whatever to get a meal.

WERE YOU EVER A PUNK? I can't say I've got a great deal of affection for that, because really, I've worked hard at playing my instrument, and perfecting at least *my* particular approach to music. And while I do say it's good fun to get up and have a thrash, to try to make a livin' out of it without properly learning your instrument . . . ah, I'm going on. It's just maybe I'm a bit old-fashioned, maybe I'm one of those boring old farts. But I really do think that you owe it to your audience to get out there and learn at *least* ten or twelve chords. And really perfect them, so that you can actually go from one chord to another without, like, doin' it one finger at a time, y'know? At least you owe them that much. So put me down as a no-go.

HOW MANY CHORDS DO YOU KNOW? Oh, Christ, I know *quite* a few, yeah. Nige shows me new ones sometimes; he gets these *downbeat* magazines and learns these jazz chords and he teaches me a few of those. But all you need is a coupla basic formations and a strong forefinger and you got it. . . . I guess you could say that about life!

WHAT KEEPS YOU AWAKE AT NIGHT WORRYING? I guess my memory—I really worry about losing my memory a lot. Because it seems to be happening, so I worry about my vanishing brain cells, I feel them sort of, like, winking out—even though I'm not doing the same sort of major self-abuse that I've done at various times in my life, even though I'm living a lot cleaner and I'm eating a lot of good food, and meeting a lot of interesting people, really taking a lot of sun. . . . Now that I'm doing all this, I should feel better, but I don't, 'cause I feel my brain cells dying. If I could only learn to communicate with the spores, you see. . .

HOW HAS YOUR LIFE CHANGED SINCE THE MOVIE CAME OUT? You mean *Indiana Jones*?

NO, *THIS IS SPINAL TAP*: Oh, that. Well, I think that we are beginning to be appreciated as a serious contender again. I think it's still in the air, though I don't particularly feel it in the employment arena. But I do feel that there's a sort of a renaissance beginning to stir, and I guess that it has to stir before it can really, you know, shake—in the words of James Bond. But I think a lot is going to change; I do know that serious critics who used to pass us off as sort of a nobody band are beginning to reemerge and, uh, say basically the same thing . . . but at least we are getting recognition once again for being p'rhaps a people's band, which is what we always were.

FIRST RECORD BOUGHT: It was an American record and I bought it from a merchant seaman who had come back from America—he used to come to our neighborhood; he lived right down the block from us—and it was "Tweedlydee" by LaVern Baker. It was just incredible. And I bought a few more from him, too: "Bony Marony" by Larry Williams and a few others like that.

FIRST CONCERT: I suppose the very first concert I ever saw, funnily enough, was a group who had just had a hit record, and it was a group that I later wound up playing for about a year after this—in 1963, it was "The Johnny Goodshow Revue." He was sort of halfway between big-band music, dance-hall music, and rock 'n' roll, because they used a lot of R&B stuff and he did have a black singer, whose name I wish I could recall. She used to do covers of LaVern Baker and that sort of thing. And then a year later I was working for him; it was very ironic, I thought.

DO YOU HAVE ANY O-LEVELS? No, I don't. I don't really think too much about that anymore.

WHAT HAVE YOU GOT IN YOUR POCKETS? I know I've got a twisted-up tissue, and I've got some American money—two quarters and a dime and four pennies—and I've got some postage stamps. . . . I'm afraid it's not very exciting. Oh, here's a little piece of chlorophyll gum, little green square of chlorophyll gum. I didn't notice it at first because it's sort of become part of the fabric of the actual pocket, so I think that's gonna stay in there until we find out some chemical way of removing it. But that's about it.

FAVORITE RONNIE PUDDING RECORD: I guess I liked "I Am the Music"—that's the only one he really had a hit with. The flip side of that wasn't bad; it was a live version of "Rubber Biscuit," which I think was recorded in Playton Hall in Moulting—they used to do a bit of live recording there. And it wasn't even the Pudding People, it was Ronnie, and a drummer—I don't really recall the names, but it was no one we liked except they really turned up a great B-side.

Taken from *Mega Hits*, November 1984

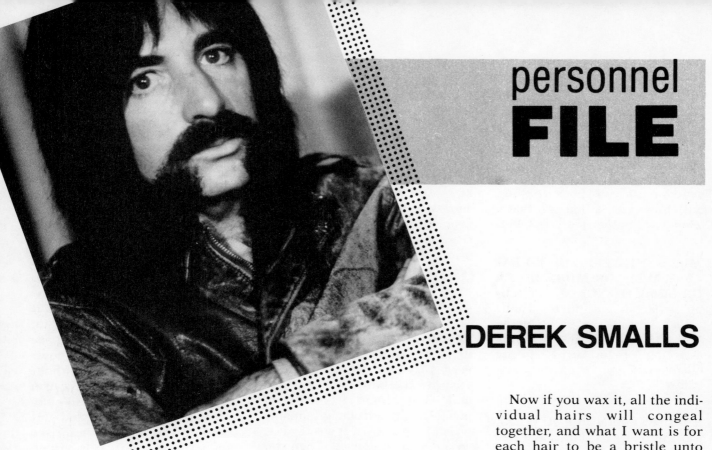

DEREK SMALLS

Now if you wax it, all the individual hairs will congeal together, and what I want is for each hair to be a bristle unto itself—each hair is a statement of bristling. It's just not a heavy metal look to have it all greased up together—that's like Sparks or somebody like that, a poufta band. So it's a wash and never, never a blow dry, just a towel dry, or a whistle through it by myself—and I'm off.

NAME: Derek Albion Smalls. As in "Isle of." Not a great deal of imagination on the part of mom and dad—it's very loyal of them.

BORN: Nilford, in the West Midlands. It had a Division Three football team that fell down to Division Four when I was a lad. I was born in 1941 as a warning to Hitler. It turned him around eventually, I believe. It took a while for him to get the message, because communications weren't so good in those days, but, you know—"Young Derek is here; watch out, Adolf!"

SCHOOLS: It was local schools—they don't call 'em "public schools" over there, because public schools are what you call "private schools"—but council schools, town schools. I didn't get past my first O-levels, which is age thirteen, and then I slagged

about a bit and when I hit seventeen I decided it was time to improve my future and I took a test and got accepted by the London School of Design.

MOUSTACHE CARE: Basically, I have a regimen that I follow rigorously, which is: After a meal, I'll scrunch up my lip to my nose, for the purpose of detecting whether the meal is still there. And if it is—that meal *or* a previous meal—then I will wash it. If not, then I will let it be. I play it by nose, you might say. Because you don't want it to soften up on you; if you wash the facial hair too often, it will droop and lose its shape. Which is not what you're looking for in a moustache of that sort. You want it to bristle up a bit. I would say maybe once every couple of days the meals begin to pile up. "Oh, yeah, there's Tuesday's eggs."

HAIR CARE: The hair is something different from the moustache, 'cause it will tangle up on you if you don't wash it. So on gig days I wash it twice: before and after. It's not a wash so much—I'll just stick me head under a sink and get the knots out. Then on non-gig days I'll just tuck it up under a hat and forget about it.

You've got to run *it*, y'know, you can't let *it* run *you*. I've had it for so long, I've just made a study of it. You don't want to deplete the oils, but you don't want 'em to dominate you. You should go to a scalpologist. I had a proper reading.

YOU HAD YOUR HAIR READ? I had my hair read. I do that about once every three months, as a matter of fact. It's the best way to tell, because if you've got a deficiency in your body, it shows up in your hair. Because your hair is your dead body—it's the dead part of your body growing out. So—what killed it? that's what a scalpologist will tell you.

MIGHT HE TELL YOU TO EAT LESS MEAT OR MORE LIVER OR SOMETHING? No one tells me what to eat, mate. That's where I draw the line. But he says, "Use an herbal, your body is crying out for herbs." In my business, it's important not to go bald.

EARLIEST BANDS YOU WERE IN: There was a kind of a bar band that I was in at the London School of Design called the Teddy Noise. It was during the Mods and Rockers era, and we were Rods. We tried to combine the two to broaden the appeal, which did *not* work, 'cause the lines were too well drawn. But it was one of the first experiments where we said, "Dash all what we *play,* just let's do it *loud."* It wasn't a concern about music for a social identity, which was big in those days. It was a power duo— me and a guitarist, and we both played very loud. The lack of a drummer was crucial to our sound, and we were faulted for our rhythmic uncertainty. But it was a very interesting experiment.

LAST BOOK READ: *How to Repair Your Own Volkswagen,* which came in handy because I bought a VW van and it went bad about two weeks later. I thought, Let's try this first before going to a professional, because it couldn't hurt. And I got about to the distributor cap and I stopped

there. But you mean read all the way through, right? Then I would say *Guide to the Hotels of Spain.* I was goin' over to Spain last year. I read all the way through and then decided, It doesn't sound too great, I'm gonna go to Jamaica instead. I don't know, there's somethin' about 'em, they just didn't sound like proper resorts to me; but I did read it all the way through. I mean, it kept my interest, it seemed well organized, and it had maps. So I would give it a C overall, maybe a C minus.

FAVORITE DRINK: It's a particular weakness of mine—just very, *very* cold Grand Marnier. Just put the bottle in the fridge and let it almost freeze. Then just take as much of it as humanly possible in one . . . It's so sweet, so strong, just *down* it. Then you are in your own Spain, so to speak.

FAVORITE DURAN DURAN RECORD: I've not really spent a lot of time listening to this haircut stuff. It all seems to be haircut music—it's like, Hey, look at our haircut! I mean, it's good synthesizer music, I *hear*—Viv tells me—but it's not what I consider rock 'n' roll, basically. Very low aggro content, which to me is crucial. "Don't You Want Me" would be my favorite if I had to pick one.

THAT'S BY THE HUMAN LEAGUE. Well, I hate to say it, but they all do look alike. A metal band or a hard-rock band —there's always a distinctive cast to the image, y'know? You can always go, "Oh, yes, that's the one with the *skull,"* or "That's the one with the *angry* skull," or "That's the one with the skull with the *horns,"* or something like that. But these

kids, it's like there's some big building in central London that they're all being bred in, like gene-splicing is going on.

WHAT TV SHOW DO YOU ALWAYS TURN OFF? In England it's "Coronation Street," 'cause it's just been goin' on *way* too long. Enough, thank you, twenty-eight years, thank you, I get it, I know it by heart. . . . Over here, "All Creatures Great and Small," because I do not like to see when the elbow goes up the pig's arse. That's it for me. Right, I'll be eatin 'im shortly and I don't want to see someone's arm up 'im, y'know? I'll have the steak, uh, without the arm, please, without the arm up the bum, if you'd be so kind, *garçon.* So I'd turn that off straightaway. And you never see him wash up afterwards, either, and then next scene he's shakin' hands with some new bloke: "'Ello, nice to see you, don't mind this, it's just been up a pig's bum." And he's always fishin' around in there—"Oh, I got one, here's your problem right here!"

PETS: I've been a fancier of snakes for some time. I have quite a large boa at home—I don't take him on the road with me because it's just too much trouble. Clarence stays at home. And I've a few more. I believe they're the most soulful of animals, snakes. I believe because of their lack of legs they're forced to be within themselves more. They cannot just go out for a stroll, so they've got to be more inward. So I do feel they're a deep animal, and they've also got that great tongue that I love, that forked tongue—lovely tongue. We tried to get one of those in the devil's head for the tour, but it just didn't work. If you get it light enough where it really looks like it's flicking, it's very hard to support it—it flies out and then it flops about; it will not stick out unless you electrify it. And then it's a whole new thing, because with the smoke and the electrification of the tongue, it's a whole new problem.

But I do love snakes, I do feel that they are my soul brothers, in a way. And there is also the slinky quality to them, which I try to apply to my stage persona. They have natural slink, of course; they don't have to wear Spandex to achieve it. It's nature's Spandex, is what they have.

WORST PERIOD IN YOUR CAREER: That period when the band broke up and were all off at loose ends. I went back to Nilford for a while, which was very depressing 'cause the mill had closed, for good. It was very sad to see people up there, and I thought, Oh, shit, what am I gonna do if I have to live *here*? I decided, No, thank you, so I did the solo album. Which was interesting because it was music with *no* melodic content. I really tried that, I really tried to just do rhythm, and harmony, and *no* melody at all. Because I felt at the time that that was the way to go; and I was wrong. But it matched my mood. That was *It's a Smalls World*.

It was also a very depressing project—nonmelodic music I find ultimately depressing. There's not a lot to feed off of, nothing to whistle, nothing to hum. It was just drone, big-beat drone music. Enough already. I almost cut my hair during that period. I *did* shave, shaved off the bars—and that was rough, 'cause I hadn't seen that lip for a while.

MOST EMBARRASSING MOMENT (Onstage): There was a number we did in the 1977 tour where I was on a trapeze rig where I spun and it got caught and suspended me for about—well, two hours after the show I was up there. I was *playin'*, mind; I had my *bass*. But it was just so stupid—I'm hangin' there and people are filin' out, throwing things at me, y'know, tossing cups of soda at me 'cause I'm just up there. . . . It was a matter of the bearings seizing up in the rigging. It was very cold up there and I was in a sort of unnatural position because of the harness: about two-thirds over on my front with my legs spread out because the harness was going through the crotch area. My balls were up around my lungs by this point. It was just like, Great, *this* is why I got into this business, to be right here like this, thank you.

I'm yelling at the top of my lungs at the roadies and they're saying, Well, Derek, we're tryin' our best, fuck you. Very nice, thank you, what a treat.

MOST EMBARRASSING MOMENT (Offstage): It was in Brighton and I was found kind of drunk, hung over, in a policewoman's uniform in a hotel lobby, and the policewoman was naked in my bedroom. It was in all the papers and there was a big, big, big . . . well, there was a little thing about it—I was supposed to have had my way with her against her will and so forth. Paradin' about the lobby, screamin', in the policewoman's skirts was a bit embarrassing. I think it was the vomit *on* the skirts that got most of the attention, though.

WOULD YOU DESCRIBE YOUR BEDROOM? Well, it's based on a Turkish theme. It's Ottoman Empire; there's about three yards of turquoise silk that hangs from the ceiling draping down, and the walls are in a burgundy silk. It's like, there's not a hard surface in the room—except for you know what. And the headboard of the bed is a burnished rosewood, kind of Chinese—I mean, it's Turkish with a Chinese rosewood nuance to it. There's the Turkish waterbed. I once tried putting Turkish coffee in it instead of water to see if it would make a difference; it was thicker liquid and made for a slower roll. The bed is kidney-shaped, custom-made.

I have a very large aquarium with some killer koi—they're bred specially for the nobles in Japan. Usually they discourage their aggressive tendencies, but my breeder breeds them to kill, so usually there is only one in the tank at any given moment. Every couple of months we'll bring in a new batch and invite some people in to watch them fight.

FAVORITE VIDEO GAME: I had Battle Zone for a while, which I was hooked on for about a year and a half, but then I got bored with it. After a year and a half, the thrill was gone, and I haven't been really sucked into one since then. But I might get back to it since it's been a while. It was sort of 3-D, but it was a weird sort of two-dimensional three-dimensionality. I had one in my den for a while.

HOW DO YOU RELAX? Well, I do a bit of amateur boxing, or I did. I don't do too much of it anymore because as you get to be in what you might call "the higher echelons of youth," which I am reaching now, it's not advisable. Nowadays, I will do a bit of gardening, actually. I don't like to talk about that too much—but I do have some splendid orchids that I'm bringing along now. I'm planning to show them in the next little while. I get kidded about it a lot, y'know, Derek and his flowers. It's supposed to be a poufta kind of activity, but I find it *very* relaxing—and they are a thing of beauty, the orchid is. You know there are more than seventeen thousand species of orchids in the world?

HAVE YOU EVER DONE ANY ACTING? Well, ever since the *Roma 79* experience, I've been bitten by the bug a little bit. You're not familiar with that over here? Marco Zamboni's *Roma 79.* During the period when the band broke up, it was one of the things I did, *before* the depression set in that I was talking about earlier. It was very exciting; it was two days' work with a director who I consider one of the most talented in the world today.

It's the first scene in the movie. I come into this hotel room, I'm dressed all in white— which is so dramatic a change for me, the fans see this and they go, "Wow, Derek's in white!" It's like a total mindfuck for them— which is the idea. When I met with Zamboni before we started shooting, he said, "I see you in white." So I'm dressed in a beautiful white suit, which I didn't get to keep.

Zamboni also made *The Sicilians (I Siciliani)*—that was an early one; *Swarthy Like Me; Fusilli for Two. Roma 79* was his epic. It was just a grand tapestry of decadence—the orgy scenes alone, which I got to hang around for after my parts were over, were like two thousand extras all dressed in Giorgio Armani clothes for this huge orgy and banquet scene. It was *modern* Rome—it was three years ahead of its time because he made it in '76.

WHEN DID YOU LAST SPEAK

TO YOUR MOTHER? About two months ago when I was home. Dad's got a bad case of the shingles, but mom's still doin' fine. It's just a kind of a chipper quality that she has: "Hello, son, how're you doin'? No, we don't need money. Your dad could use a call at the hospital." That sort of thing. And I will call him.

LAST RECORD BOUGHT: Bought? Get off it. I mean, I have connections through the company.

OK, LAST RECORD ACQUIRED, THEN. *Songs of the Solomon Islands.* I'm very deeply into Polynesian music—mus*ics*, plural, because each island has a different kind of music—and, of course, it's very *beat*-oriented. A very rhythmic quality. I can take licks off 'em, just directly translate 'em, because they're very repetitive—no one will know. *No one will know.* Because if you try to cop a lick from some *band*, you get nicked right away, but these are just there for the taking. I don't know why more people haven't thought of it, actually.

STRANGEST GIFT FROM A FAN: I would say a live frog. I got one once from a girl, backstage in Cleveland. The message that accompanied the frog just said, "There's more where this came from." Which I didn't understand at all—and I didn't want to find out what it meant. And then whaddaya do, do you throw it away? I left it in the toilet of the club, actually. I certainly didn't want to meet the girl who sent me the frog—there was some message there that I didn't find quite appropriate.

WHAT DO YOU WEAR TO BED? Normally, Chinese silk pajamas. In very hot weather, swim trunks. They would be silk swim

trunks, yes. And then occasionally, a silk nothing—*au naturel,* if you will. But normally I'm a pajama man; there's something about it that reminds me of my days as a child. I was a pajama child, so . . . . the pajama child is father of the pajama man.

FAVORITE APPLIANCE: Besides my hair dryer? ACCU-JAC I guess would be my favorite appliance. For those moments between—well, for those moments between.

WHAT DO YOU DO WITH AN ACCU-JAC? Use it as directed. Are you familiar with it? It is an aid to the giving of pleasure to one's male self. It's a remarkably lifelike simulation, is all I can say, and in some cases—no, I don't want to say better than the real thing, but it gets frighteningly close sometimes. Always the real thing first, of course. But in those moments between . . . ACCU-JAC.

DO YOU BELIEVE IN ASTROLOGY? No, that's rubbish. Now, I don't want to say rubbish, because David believes in it so wholeheartedly, but . . . I believe in a cosmology, I believe in a philology—it's not a philosophy, it's a study of a philosophy. And I believe in heaven and hell, of course—I would be a hypocrite if I didn't, because we are depicting that so often in our music. I believe in the spirit world, the power of healers to heal, out-of-body experiences. I believe in extraterrestrial life. I believe in a civilization that once flourished on the continent of Atlantis, which had achieved space travel and communication with other planets. I believe that other beings have visited here and made contact with us in previous lifetimes. I believe in reincarnation—I *was* a Mayan prince. So, those are a few of the beliefs I cherish. But, you know, astrology is such a load of rubbish. Don't quote me on that, because David gets upset, but it's such a joke.

IS THERE A BASIC DIFFERENCE BETWEEN YOU AND THE OTHER MEMBERS OF THE BAND WHEN IT COMES TO THE SPIRITUAL? I believe in contacting the spirits through certain processes, certain ways of being, mystical states. But basically, I feel I'm a more rational, logical kind of person than David or Nigel. I'm in *this* world more than they are, I think, although, as I say, I was a Mayan prince, in *that* world. But now I am in *this* world, you see what I'm saying? I'm able to be *in* this world *with* the knowledge that I once existed in *that* world. In this world I deal as a rational, logical person; in that world I dealt the way a Mayan prince deals with the world—*that* world. Magical processes then, but not now, you see. One adapts, doesn't one? Or perishes.

WERE YOU EVER A HIPPIE? Yeah, I guess I was if you mean did I smoke enormous amounts of high-quality hashish and sleep with every girl who had hair longer than her shoulders. I wasn't a hippie in the sense that I wasn't going to a lot of rock festivals and sitting on the grass and falling asleep and waking up the next morning to find myself under two feet of mud. Not *that* kind of hippie. I was on stage; I was the person who was drawing them *into* the mud. I was the mud-magnet!

But if you mean a believer in a sort of mushy kind of peace and love and free concerts, no. We *never* did free concerts. We were never a hippie band in that sense, although if you look back,

"Flower People" was a hippie statement. It was saying there is something better—not specifically noting *what*, which I think was wise on our part. We weren't saying, "We know the way," on *that* record. I think we were saying, "Stay tuned for later records; we might find the way."

WERE YOU EVER A PUNK? No, that goes without saying. I mean, we have none of us been a follower of fashion. We have tried in our way to *mold* fashion. Yes, we did go through a glam period, about four years later than everybody else—but that was because we were trying to start it all *over* again. It's a different mind-set. It's not followership—it's late leadership.

WOULDN'T SOME PEOPLE JUST CALL THAT REVIVALISM? Well, yeah, I guess they would. But it wasn't out of nostalgia. The previous couple of albums hadn't sold too well, you see. And we felt—or our people, our manager before Ian [Faith], Evan MacGregor, felt—that this was the way to go. So it wasn't out of nostalgia, it was out of greed, I guess you *could* say. Let's be honest: Nobody ever said we were in rock 'n' roll to be poor, not even in the hippie days. That's why we never did free concerts, for example. Because we said, "Right, you give us free instruments and free air travel and free blue jeans and free paisley dashikis, and we'll give you free concerts." That's what I mean about a rational, logical approach to it, not woolly-headed.

WHAT KEEPS YOU AWAKE AT NIGHT WORRYING? Coffee.

YOU WORRY ABOUT COFFEE? Yeah . . . No, I mean that's what keeps me awake at night—you

have any after ten at night and that's it. But that's where the cold Grand Marnier comes in handy. I keep a pitcher of it in the fridge and then it's no worries for Derek, no being kept awake in bed tonight, *dear!*

But you mean—well, nuclear. If you're talking about being sober at bedtime, I *could* be kept awake by that stuff if I were sober. I'm fantasizing now. Y'know, the future. My view of it is, No use worrying about the past: done. Done. Worry about the future, ducks. That's where it's gonna be at. Let's put it this way: on a night where I remembered actually getting *into* bed, if I were awake that long, I would worry about the future.

FIRST RECORD BOUGHT: "It's My Party," Lesley Gore.

FIRST CONCERT: Lonnie Donegan. I was big into skiffle—as a consumer, not as a producer of it. David and Nigel were on the other end of it from me. Nige, he was the king of skiffle for a while—big deal, King of Skiffle, but . . .

FAVORITE URIAH HEEP RECORD: *Abominog,* mainly because I like it the way it's said backwards: *Gonimoba.* I like that. It's a quasi palindrome, which has a mystical component to it. Also, I admire it as a comeback record, because I would say that about half the records we made have been of that genre. So I admire that in other bands.

DID YOU LIKE *GREMLINS*? That's the one with the little creatures? Yeah, I saw the coming attractions for 'em, but I didn't go to see the movie; I basically go to see movies that have more snakes in them than that, because of my herpetology bent.

HOW HAS YOUR LIFE CHANGED SINCE THE MOVIE CAME OUT? I got divorced, and therefore am a bit poorer for the experience. I do not have the Lamborghini anymore—I was left with the Mini. She also got the satellite dish and a few other things, but we're still on very good terms. As a matter of fact, at the end of the Japanese tour after the movie had been filmed —the Sex Farm Tour—Pamela was quitting modeling and forming her own band and she said, "Derek, if things aren't going well with Tap and you want to come audition for me, you're more than welcome." So it's very amiable.

I think we're more recognizable—not more recognized but more recogniz*able*. They're coming—well, they're actually coming *near* me in the street, they're not coming quite *up* to me yet. They're almost veering towards me and then changing their minds and veering away. So in that sense it's not a problem yet. There's just a smattering of adulation, which I feel is the sincerest form of smattering.

DO YOU BREAKDANCE? Get off it! I feel a white man breakdancing is an affront. That's not a racialist statement, it's just a matter of taste. It doesn't belong to us. It's like if you saw a black man speaking Swedish, same thing.

OR, SAY, A BLACK HEAVY METAL BAND? Right, *right.* First of all—and I don't mean to be racialist again, but the hair— what would we do with the hair? Dreadlocks would not work, that would not be the look. Then you're talking about great amounts of time spent under hot irons with very, very caustic chemicals, which I think could be a drag in the long run for them. Or wigs, which would be a bit stupid. Tina Turner, though, did it, so you never know. It *could* happen. That's why you have to worry about the future so much!

WHAT HAVE YOU GOT IN YOUR POCKETS? I've got shorts on . . . let's see. I've got a nice little wad of some of Morocco's best, and I have some bubble gum. Matches; some ashes from Morocco's best of last night; the phone number of a girl named Candy. Which is my little system anyway—I mean, it's odd that I would actually meet up with a girl named Candy, because for convenience's sake I tend to call all of 'em Candy. It's a complimentary name, and they feel flattered by it, y'know.

A couple of these stupid coins they have over here, these little thin ones?

DIMES? Yeah, with the funny edges. They make great screwdrivers is basically what I found they're good for. We don't have a coin in England that really can serve that purpose, so if you're lacking a screwdriver you're out of luck. But over here—I guess this is a more handy country in that sense. I have a piece of skin from Clarence, my boa, from his last molting. I keep it with me just to remember him by. . . .

SORT OF A KEEPSNAKE? Keepsnake! Good, that's a good one!

FAVORITE RONNIE PUDDING RECORD: Well, "I Am More Music" would have to be it because basically if you look at the thing rationally, he only did *one.* He's not my favorite bass player, it goes without saying, but there's no hard feelings. I mean, it was the break of my career for him to leave Tap.

PERSONAL MOTTO: I *would* like my epitaph to be what I said before: "Not a woolly-head." Which is as close as I come to a motto, in terms of how I try to live my life. "Fuck my ex-wife's lawyer" might be my motto at this stage of the game.

Taken from *Mega Hits*, January 1985

THE BEAT GOES ON

Rock and Roll Simulation

A Hollywood agent and a male vocalist were indicted by a federal grand jury for impersonating Spinal Tap, it was reported last month.

The lid was lifted on the ruse that's been successful for the last five years when the phony group was playing gigs in Phoenix and Valparaiso last May while the real Spinal Tap were appearing before upwards of 2,000 fans at Ron Delsener's Palladium in New York.

Distance wasn't the only thing that separated the bogus group from the real thing. According to Roger Grade, attorney for the real Spinal Tap, "The imitators fooled a lot of people except that Spinal Tap are British and sometimes the guys in the other group had Australian and even American accents—the pseudo-personnel changed from time to time."

Grade was quoted by Bill Wechsler in the *New York Daily News* as saying, "A lot of people really thought they were the real Spinal Tap, although many others said 'They sound better than they used to.'"

According to Wechsler, the indictment alleges that the non-Taps received $3,500 (total) for three shows at Fort Monmouth and Fort Dix, New Jersey, last March. Attorney Grade said that some nightclubs that booked the imitators called him "to ask why

Nigel Tufnel cleans the wax out of his ears after being told about all those free meals consumed in his name.

Spinal Tap were charging so much." He noted that the real Spinal Tap, whose string of hits in the Sixties was limited to "Gimme Some Money" and "(Listen to the) Flower People," make "substantially less than $1,200 a night."

The two persons named in the indictment were Larry Barth, who runs a booking company called Creative International Artists (CIA), and Manny Gorecki, lead singer of the un-Spinals. They were charged with conspiracy to defraud by mailing promotional literature to nightclubs and bars offering Spinal Tap.

Gimme Some More Money

In an apparently unrelated incident, a man has been arrested and charged with fraud after posing as Spinal Tap guitarist Nigel Tufnel for a period of months, during which time he cashed checks, obtained free meals and drinks at local restaurants, and, in at least one instance, received the favors of a group of teenage girls.

Authorities in Normal, Illinois, said that they were holding the impostor, whom they identified as Philip Schiff. Suspicions were aroused when the apocryphal Nigel repeatedly turned down requests to sing Spinal Tap favorites at a couple of the bars where he was receiving free drinks, claiming that he "couldn't remember the words." Instead, he insisted on singing some songs of his own, which he insisted were "new Tap compositions" not yet recorded. Normal Deputy Sheriff Lance Macklin remarked, however, that the so-called "new" songs were neither as rough nor as simplistic as those previously associated with Spinal Tap.

"You could tell *this* fellow had a real knack for singing. Besides, the songs themselves had all kinds of neat little hooks and catchy parts—like a real pop song you hear on the radio would have." Although Macklin admitted he was not "intimately familiar" with Tap's recorded output, he said that he "had heard enough to know there wasn't that much to it."

Reached in Squatney, London, where Spinal Tap were busy preparing for their forthcoming tour of America (on the heels of "Nice 'n' Stinky," their surprise hit off the two-year-old *Jap Habit* LP), Tufnel was noncommittal at first. But when it was suggested that the impostor's actions could have a negative effect on Tap's American tour by creating ill will here, the guitarist's attitude changed to an irritated "No comment."

Excerpt from *Screem*, July 1977

SPINAL RAP:

DAVID and DEREK COME CLEAN

Even the heavy-duty, murderous schedules of proto-rockers like Genghis Khan and Attila the Hun would loom a bit limp alongside the recent Spinal Tap World Tour, particularly the Japanese and American branches. Nigel Tufnel, Derek Smalls, David St. Hubbins, Viv Savage, and Ric Shrimpton have embarked on a mobile global extravaganza that could easily leave them gasping for air somewhere between Upper Volta and Lower Slobovia when it finally grinds to a halt sometime next year. They've been in North America so long, in fact, that David St. Hubbins has taken up part-time residence in southern California (where he claims there are more British rock personnel than in all of London!), and Nigel Tufnel's once incomprehensible Squatney accent is threatening to become merely arcane.

Spinal Tap was formed in that same part of London's East End almost twenty years ago, but it wasn't till the surprising (and, some felt, egregiously overdue) success of "Nice 'n' Stinky" from the redoubtable *Jap Habit* LP that Tap brought the male-dominated world of metal fans to its collective knees. (It was almost enough to make us forgive them the ill-advised packaging gimmick of including those sushi-sized bits of real raw tuna in the British import version, to be sure.)

Throughout its headthumping history, Spinal Tap has created a modicum of controversy. Critics call the band tuneless, tasteless, and derivative. Photographers and picture editors bemoan Derek Smalls's unshaven appearance and chronically misproportioned moustache. Fellow musicians lash out at Tap, though rarely by name. One big-name band that headlined for them on a previous tour claims that Tap kept girls away from the box office, while a member of yet another rival band scoffs that the Tufnel/St. Hubbins guitar setup looks and sounds suspiciously like Judas Priest's. But Tap have continued on, undaunted and unafraid.

On a break from mixing their forthcoming, as yet untitled album, two of Tap's three main men cleaned their breasts of a number of vexing matters *(and not a small amount of hair—Ed.)*. What follows is a slapdash reconstruction of their comments.

I wonder if you could say a few words about your producer of so many years, Glyn Hampton-Cross?
DAVID: He was a very interesting bloke. He used to work as an office boy or a sort of a runner at Megaphone, where we first released our, um, first releases. We got to know him around that time, and he was very smart, and big. And when you're big, people think of you as being *not* smart, they don't expect you to be really smarter than them. They treat you like, Oh, here's a big bloke, I'll be sure not to hurt his feelings or anything, he might kill me. But it turned out that he was busy double-thinkin' them all the time, he was always one step ahead. There was a time there when it looked like he was gonna be head of Megaphone itself, but it didn't work out. He wound up just being head of A & R—Artists and Repertoire—and he did most of our production as the Thamesmen all the way through Spinal Tap, up until, I guess, the early Seventies.

I know he did the live album, the *Jap Habit* album, but I'm not really sure. I think he was there for some of *The Sun Never Sweats*, but we did part ways, mostly because he was more interested in a different kind of sound, I think. I think we were going for a more hard sound, like the twin guitar leads and things like that. What he wanted to do was build our audience, make it broader, so he was gonna start bringin' in, like, we were gonna do Broadway show tunes. I thought it was a bum idea, frankly. And it was a bit of a parting of the ways . . . and so that's it. Nice bloke.

Any idea whatever became of him?
DAVID: I don't really know. He was a family man, and I do know that he had some land in Iceland. I don't know if that helps anyone, I just know that he'd pop up to Reykjavik every now and then with his wife and his daughters—he's got a coupla little girls. She's Icelandic. I think maybe they might've settled down up there, I don't really know.

Plagiarism is a serious problem in the world of pop music. For example, one of the other metal publications recently carried an interview with a rival band of yours, Judas Priest—
DEREK: Oh, come on, they're not rivals. They're doing a different thing, they're doing a very simple, basic bit; they're where we were at ten or twelve years ago.

Then how would you say Spinal Tap has evolved differently over those years?
DEREK: Well, I mean, you don't find Judas Priest doin' suites, do ya? Like "Stonehenge," that's a fuckin' suite, innit?

But it's only one song.
DEREK: No, but it's got three different melodies—that's a suite.

Usually you think of suites as complex things that go on for fifteen or twenty minutes, don't you?
DAVID: Yeah, well we do short suites. Short 'n' suite.

OK. But on their new album, *Defenders of the Faith*, Priest do a song called "Heavy Duty." How do you feel about that? And are you planning any legal action?
DEREK: *Really?* "Heavy Duty"? Now if we could afford a solicitor, I'm sure we would. But they charge you right off the bat. It's like, "If you want to get money out of them, you've got to give us money first"—which doesn't seem to me like the best way to go. We'll probably just slag it out with the boys when we see 'em next time.

Lead singer Rob Halford goes on at length to explain the album's title, *Defenders of the Faith*—that the faith is heavy metal and that they're defending it against, well, anyone who would put it down, I guess.
DEREK: Well, see, this is what I find deficient about them is their insistence on overcoherence. It's like they've got to explain everything, you know? I mean, if you have to explain it, why do it? That's my—I wouldn't call it a philosophy, but my philately, I guess I would call it.

They refer to Halford as "heavy metal's intelligent defender." What do you think of that?
DAVID: Who? Rob Halford? Yeah, well, there you go. What's he doin' playin' heavy metal music, then? He's slummin', that's what he's doin'.

Derek, can you tell us why you dropped out of the pop music scene in 1965 and enrolled in the London School of Design?
DEREK: Well, I feel it walked away from me a bit. But I would also say I misread the situation; I thought that British music was sort of on the wane and was not going to be something with any staying power. I just totally misread the situation—I thought it was not a growth situation to be in and I'd better get out while the getting was good. I felt advertising's gonna *be* there. My dad said to me, "Der, advertising will always *be* there, there will always be advertising until the Russians take over—and maybe even *they*'ll do advertising." But it wasn't his fault. I was doing my own reading of the situation, and in retrospect it proved out to be an incorrect one.

Could you explain why Spinal Tap never played Woodstock? Were you just not invited?
DEREK: We weren't invited, were we? You look at the list of acts at Woodstock, and how many of them were non-American? Joe Cocker wasn't strictly speaking American, but he was doing an American style of music, wasn't he? "Oh, I'll be like your soul singers, won't I?" But who else? Not very many, I wager you—it was love, peace, and Yanks. "Woodstock Festival of Love, Peace, and Yanks" is what we called it. But of course we did our share of festivals. We did, as you know, the Isle of Lucy Festival.

I heard a rumor that Marco Zamboni, the Italian director in whose film, *Roma 79*, you appeared briefly, was going to do Tap's next video. True?
DEREK: Well, *I* keep telling the band that we should get him to

do our videos, but, y'know, try to tell these geezers somethin' and it's like, Oh, yeah, thank you very much, Derek, go back to your bass now and let the geniuses work!

Kind of like being the Ringo Starr of the band—or the George Harrison.
DAVID: Kind of like being the Daley Thompson of the Olympics, y'know? Maybe the show is great, wins the decathlon, but doesn't get any airtime. How much did you see *him*?

What do you think of the "cult" metal bands such as Anthrax, Hellhammer, Metallica, and others?
DEREK: Oh, they're all right— for what they're doing, it's fine. It's fourth-generation kind of stuff—they've obviously listened to us, which is a compliment, it's the sincerest form of listening. We're pleased that the younger bands see something in us that they choose to emulate and refine and make their own, even if it is still, basically, ours. More power to them, I say, I really do. We have a different mission, which is not to preach to the converted. You know, Judas Priest talks about "defending the faith," whatever that is. We're *extending* the faith, so to speak: "Extenders of the Faith." We're faith-extenders, that's what I feel. What we have to sell is more important than what *they* have to sell.

What exactly are you selling?
DEREK: Music, records, tapes . . . ourselves . . . our very souls.

Selling yourselves—you admit that it's come to that?
DEREK: It always *was* that. I think we've been very realistic about our position in the music business; I think we always realized it's a business—they don't call it the "music fun," y'know, they call it the "music business." They never call it the "music picnic." I think we've always been aware that it was called the "music business."

That sounds like a Sixties band, doesn't it.
DEREK: The Music Picnic? It does, doesn't it?

Their first single would be "Where's the Ants?"
DEREK: "Where's the Pickles?" would be their second.

Taken from *Zoo*, October 1984

GUITAR STARS

DAVID ST. HUBBINS

by F. S. Gotterfunken

(Photos by Steve Meltzer.)

While some guitarists are not content to merely rely upon their skills as great axemen but feel compelled to cover any lapses by cavorting wildly around the stage, yet others more secure in the knowledge of their own irreconcilable greatness are able to hold their ground and simply *play their asses off!* David St. Hubbins, long the guitarist-vocalist *extraordinaire* with Spinal Tap, belongs to neither of these classifications. For he is alone unto himself.

Though his guitar playing is often lost in the shadow of the stolidly flamboyant Nigel Tufnel, it remains a potent if often overlooked aspect of the band's success. On a typical night we might see St. Hubbins striding the stage in his trademark white Adidas (the Patron Saint of Quality Footwear, indeed!), taking a restrained leap in the air, or firing off a string of tautly strummed chords—all

within the space of only a few minutes.

But what of the quietly smiling man behind the white Gibson SG that has become his trademark? What thoughts pass through the fervid mind concealed within this otherwise benign exterior? These questions and more nudged my brain as I tracked David down at his new temporary digs—a mellow, southern Californian villa he's renting while Tap is gracing (pounding?) America with their heavy presence.

HIT STREAM: When did you first start playing guitar?
DAVID ST. HUBBINS: I was about—oh, Christ, twelve or thirteen, I suppose. My first guitar was a four-string tenor guitar by Nibbleng, a German make. It was a bit embarrassing, I had to scrape the picture of the Kingston Trio off the side. They had a picture of the whole trio right there near the pick guard and I had to sort of sand it down,

so there was a sort of white spot there. It was just this crummy little guitar, but I had a great time learning it. Of course, later on I had to learn what to do with the other two strings. I mostly played in the key of C or G, just because I could reach the chords without having to barre anything. Small hands, y'know?

HS: Do you remember *why* guitar?
DSH: Well, it was the most *portable* of all the instruments, I think, with the exception of vocals, which are extremely portable, I s'pose—almost built-in, innit? So portability, and af*ford*ability, because this only cost me about eight pounds. I got it through a mate who knew someone at the warehouse at Stockby's who got a great deal on 'em. My first set of strings? I think I pinched 'em. I just waltzed into the music store and waltzed out again with a set of strings. They were the wrong size strings for the guitar, they were like very

difficult to play, but it didn't really matter.

HS: Did you have any formal musical training?

DSH: Not really. I s'pose you could say, my dad loved opera and he'd play classical records and opera. So I'd be sittin' readin' the *Beano*—you don't know what the *Beano is,* do you? It's like a monthly comic magazine—he'd be playin' a record and a bit would come up he'd like me to hear, y'know? He'd just reach out, smack me on the back of the head, and say, "'ere! Listen t' this bit 'ere!" But as far as formal training, I guess you'd have to say I learned as I went.

HS: What do you consider your trademark guitar?

DSH: Right now mostly I'm playing the white Gibson SG, which I bought just before going to America for the first time. It's still my number one guitar. I've had work done on it, I've had one of the pickups replaced, but that's my main guitar. It's got a little astrological symbol up at the top, y'know; it's a nice guitar, I don't think I could live without it. I'm not a big collector of guitars, but I also have a Les Paul Deluxe, which was a gift from an American rock star who for legal reasons I can't mention his name, but it's a bit heavy for me. I've got a Fender Telecaster, and that's been decorated with Johnson and Johnson adhesive tape; and my Gibson J-160, which is an acoustic-electric. I've had that since 1965. I just had it redone, had the pickups rewired and such. My first electric guitar was a JimElectro—not a DanElectro, which was a fairly famous name; I believe it's his brother or something. My first amplifier was a Blondel; they don't make 'em anymore.

It's a German amp, Blondel seven-watt Super-Beatnik, and they don't make *those* anymore, for obvious reasons. It's great for playin' in a living room or something. But in those days, kids hadn't built up the resistance that they have these days. These days, kids are *born* needing louder music. At the time, rock 'n' roll had to be a bit louder than anything else, but what we had to be a bit louder than was a *piano.* So seven watts was enough.

HS: The Gibson SG is sort of a trademark of Angus Young from AC/DC. Was there an influence one way or the other?

DSH: I really don't like to say that. They've been around for a number of years as well, since the early Seventies. And I can't really come out and say, "Yes, Angus was influenced by me," because our playing is not that similar really. He's mostly a lead jammer; myself, I'm mostly rhythm guitar. But I think that Angus has definitely carried on the tradition of SG as ultimate rock instrument. I admire his playing very much, and, of course, I admire his whole stage outlook—he seems to be not takin' himself too seriously and just havin' a great time.

HS: How about his stage outfit? That schoolboy gear?

DSH: I like that, too. Personally, I couldn't wear something like that—it wouldn't be quite right for me—but it works for him and that's fine. He's Australian, after all—that has to be taken into account no matter *what* you talk about.

HS: With all this rivalry between the Brits and the Aussies, what do you *really* think about metallers from down under?

DSH: I don't want to tar them all with the same brush, y'know? I *do* feel that there are some bandwagon jumpers, you know what I mean? But that's on either side of the world. I think people do tend to think of Australians as just sort of fake Englishmen—which I suppose might hold water in some quarters. But I don't really like to think that way, because they're human beings and they can't help it if they started as a prison society. I mean, so did Detroit, for that matter—and, of course, Detroit *looks* it. No, I like Aussies, I do, I do. . . . I like Kiwis, too. I've been to New Zealand a few times. It's a great country; you've got to say things to them three or four times before they even say "Wha?" But once you get through to them, you can get them to buy you drinks and everything; they're fine people, really.

HS: What kind of strings do you favor, any particular brand or type?

DSH: You know what I do? I take it down to the shop; I say, "You pick. Your choice." They put strings on and I don't ask, really. Once they put 'em on the guitar, there's no tags hangin' off 'em sayin', "This is what kind of strings you're playin'." As long as it gets through two shows without breakin' a string, I'm fine.

HS: How about effects boxes, fuzztones, that kind of thing?

DSH: I've got one that's still in experimental form—it's called the Blanc Box. It was developed by Mel Blanc, who does all the voices for the Warner Brothers cartoons. It doesn't really work great yet, but you play through this and it makes the guitar sound like it's doing the voice of, y'know, the Tasmanian Devil or Daffy Duck. It doesn't work too well with keyboards, but as far as playing single-note lines on the guitar, it's very interesting. I hope they perfect it soon.

HS: Do you have a favorite kind of pick?
DSH: Sort of a medium-gauge pick—we have picks made up for us by a bloke in Oakland, California, Spinal Tap picks. Actually we're long overdue—he gave us a couple of gross about six months ago and they're about gone now. When we were first with Polymer, right before the release of *Shark Sandwich*, they had a bunch of picks made up for us with the Spinal Tap logo on one side, and on the other side of the pick it had an actual thumbprint that was mine on the ones that were for me, or Nige's thumbprint on his. It was really great just to know that you had your thumb resting on your very own thumbprint—it was nice. It didn't slip, either, because it had these grooves that were matchin' up with yours. And not anyone else could play them—anyone else would pick one up and try to play, it'd fly right out of his hand, y'know. It was a nice touch, we were gratified.

HS: What would you say is your finest moment on record?
DSH: It would have to be the *Silent But Deadly* album. We were just developing ourselves as a more loose, boogie-oriented jam group—there's a long cut about eighteen or nineteen minutes called "Short 'n' Easy," and Nige and I really cut loose on that one, playing in tandem, one after the other. It still holds up, too: I heard a bit of it used recently as one of those things when they show on the telly, y'know, "We'll be right back with

more news." They played a bit of that and it really held up nice.

HS: It's been a while since your last live album and your fans would probably like another one. Any plans?
DSH: We talked about doing a cable-TV special and releasing the sound track to that. Don't recall what happened. Now that we seem to be drawing a bit better and people in the States seem to be more aware of us, p'rhaps the time is ripe. The film *[This Is Spinal Tap]* just opened in the U.K. this past Wednesday, and I wouldn't be surprised if people were sort of reminded that we exist. Which is the first step to making a comeback, innit? A comeback has to start with "Whatever-happened-to...?" And if you don't really remember *who* it happened to, whatever it was, then you're not gonna want a comeback. Even a journey like a comeback starts with a single step, y'know?

HS: How much do you practice?
DSH: I practice sort of absent-mindedly. I'll sit and I'll watch telly, or I'll be outside talkin' on the phone or sitting by the tub—they got a hot tub here, y'know, though I don't go in much 'cause I'm sort of pale, but I like the bubbling sounds. So I sit around *by* the hot tub, in the shade, and I sort of play absently—I don't even plug in. It's an electric guitar, but I just play at it without plugging in.

HS: Have you ever considered the longevity of Spinal Tap?
DSH: Well, yeah, I guess you can't help it, can you? If you're a group and you're together more than six months, longevity does enter into it. We're very proud of the fact that, come what may, hell or high water—*mostly* hell

—we seem to be hanging in there. We've come to near-splits many times: 'Seventy-six through 'eight were very, very slow times. We almost split up. We said to each other, "Look, let's not spend any time together unless it's absolutely necessary, unless there's a real clamoring for Spinal Tap product"—and there *wasn't*.

Tell you the truth, I became sort of a gadfly, I became more of a figure than a performer. "Who was at the party, who was liggin' about backstage?" "Well, David St. Hubbins was there...." I was everywhere, but I wasn't doing anything.

HS: Sort of Richard Burton syndrome, eh?
DSH: Yes, very much so, yeah. Rest his soul. And mine, as well! But around that time I met Jeanine and she said, "What the fuck you doin'? I always see you at these things, you're always there stuffing cold cuts in your face and drinkin' vodka and lime and what have you...." So I began playin' a bit more and writing; writing on my own was always difficult for me—I'd usually be takin' it from Nige.

So you talk about longevity, yes, this group has been together in one sense or another since 1964. That's twenty years. There were times when it got to you, but we decided to hang in and here we are, we're back. We've never really been away, but we're back.

HS: Has near-success changed your life-style, then?
DSH: Yeah, I think it has. Now when I walk into the Rainbow or On the Rocks, they know who I am. I'm not just a trivia question anymore—well, actually, I am, but I'm a *current* trivia question. It's nice; it's nice to see your

peers and they come up to you and say, "Oh, I saw you on 'Pop, Look and Listen' twenty years ago," or "I went to Altamont in 1969 to hear you, and you didn't show up!" Which is just as well, in my opinion. We were booked on that bill as well, but some plane connection or something . . . It was a disappointment at the time, until we found out how poorly it went. Of course, we weren't headliners, y'know—there only would've been a *maiming* during *our* set.

HS: Could you pick out an example of one of your favorite guitar techniques on record and maybe explain it for our guitar-playing readers?
DSH: I don't really know how specific I can get, except that one of my major inspirations, as far as the technique of playing, has always been Sam Peckinpah, the director. It's just the way he had of sort of bending time. He'd go into slo-mo when something extremely fast was happening. It's like, I *think* in slow motion when I'm playing, and it helps me —because I know I'm not a flash guitarist. Therefore when I'm doing things, I'm doing it in a different time than you're hearing it—I put myself into the zone. I know I do a lot of bending, a lot of hammering on; but again, I think the more important things for me are the rhythm parts because they're set and I play them the same each time.

HS: What thoughts run through your mind when you're playing a solo onstage?
DSH: Mostly not thoughts so much as numbers. I'll go, like, I've got eight bars this time, so I think, One, two, three, four, all the way up to eight. Eight is my signal to stop and let someone else take over. Because I know

that once my solo stops, Nigel's generally starts—and then I can think about anything I want!

But I do think about communication. I do think the most important thing, whether you're singing or playing or just standing there clapping your hands over your head, you are communicating with a huge, multi-brained organism out there. You can't communicate with them individually, because it would take you all day, so you try to see all these faces as one face. And if that face has a pair of ears in working order—better still.

Toward the end of the set, I'm thinking more about, like, sangria, and maybe a shower, citrus fruit and vodka—toward the end of a set, I find that my thoughts get more specific, and they usually have to do with relief. I'm thirty-something years old and it's not as easy as it was. I think the time to have really wild and unkempt thoughts is when you're in your twenties. You get more practical. I find I start thinking in terms of B-1 injections, things like that, rather than cosmic truth.

HS: It's a matter of circulation, isn't it?
DSH: Yes. In fact, that's why I jump up and down onstage. It's not that I'm trying to be trendy and pogo—my feet fall asleep on stage. I wear these orthopedic boxing shoes and they help a bit. But you've gotta keep going—your ass could fall asleep if you're not careful.

HS: Is it difficult to sing and play guitar at the same time?
DSH: Not for me. We design the songs that way: David's not gonna play anything fancy here, 'cause he's singing this bit.

HS: Do you ever employ back-

ward masking on your records?
DSH: Not to my knowledge, no. All our records are carefully screened in that regard. In "Christmas with the Devil" there is a message *from* the devil, but it's not backward masking—it's there, it's all there.

HS: What's the message?
DSH: Well, I'm not gonna tell you, you gotta find it for yourself. It's very clear; it's very simple, as a matter of fact. You've gotta listen carefully, but it's not masked in any way.

HS: If you *could* use backward masking, what message would you put there?
DSH: I s'pose if there *were* any message I'd want, it would be "Turn the fuckin' thing around and play it the right way, schmuck!" It would be interestin' to put that in as a message —you play it backward and it says, "Hey, you're playin' the fuckin' record backward! What's the matter with you! Turn it around and do it right, or don't do it at all. Or trade it in for Huey Lewis and the News." It's like, if you want us, play us right. I s'pose that would be it.

I'm not a Satanist myself. Derek dabbles a bit. You go to his flat in London and he'll show up at the door wearin' a fuckin' hood or something, y'know. So it's not really my thing—it's a nice hood, though; it's got these double cutaways and it's nice. But I've got no Satanist message to transmit.

HS: You've never tried to advance your career by calling on the name of the devil, then?
DSH: No. I might give it a try someday, though, if things get a bit slow again. I used to call on the name of Remy Martin quite a

bit when things got slow, y'know —Johnny Walker, Glen Livet, things like that. *They* certainly didn't help too much. I mean, they kept you a bit loose and they made unemployment a bit more enjoyable. But then again, if your tastes run to Remy Martin, you've got to have someone supporting you if you're not employed.

HS: There's a curiously familiar classical riff at the end of "Heavy Duty"—where is it from and who was responsible for it? **DSH:** Oh, yeah—well, I dunno. That's the Barcarolle bit or somethin', I s'pose. No, I don't really remember; it's just somethin' we came up with. But I don't knock classical music. Far from it. I mean, it's nice to be tied up in all this, you know. It's now, it's what's happening, it's todaysville and all that shit. But it's important to look back. I've got an extensive Glenn Miller collection here, and you would hardly think that someone who makes his living behaving as *I* do would go for Glenn Miller. But there's a great great beat to it *and* there's great lyrics even though it's mostly known as an instrumental big band. There's a great song called "Pennsylvania 6-5000," and that's virtually the only lyric in the song. But that's very rock 'n' roll, innit? It's got that same sort of thing, y'know, as "Tequila!"—that kind of simple refrain. So I just think that kids shouldn't ace themselves out, because there's a lot of great music out there—classical music, jazz, Congolese drummers, stuff like that. Don't limit yourself.

HS: It's like that guy says on TV, I guess: So many of our most popular melodies are based on the classics. . . . **DSH:** That's right, yes! John Williams, the actor. He's been dead for, like, six years now, and he's still doin' that bloody commercial! Now that's what I call longevity. You were talkin' about longevity before—I would like to be still gigging extensively when I'm four years dead, like this bloke. And I just hope that the film *This Is Spinal Tap* has done something to facilitate that. Look at Elvis Presley—I mean, this bloke's bigger than ever and he's been dead since 'seventy-seven. And he's *huge!* Jim Morrison. Laurel and Hardy had a hit record in the U.K. three years ago: "Tale of the Lonesome Pine" was in the Top Ten. So don't give up. That's my advice to you, to any rock 'n' roller starting out. They want to know, Is this for me? I don't know if it's for you or not. Give it a try. You might wind up working like a bastard when you're dead!

It's like I always used to say: Rock 'n' roll keeps ya young— but ya *die* young.

Taken from *Hit Stream*, July–August 1984

GUITAR STARS

NIGEL TUFNEL

by Mark Molinara

(Photos by Steve Meltzer.)

When rock's top guitarists get together to discuss their craft, one name that bears a better than even chance of being mentioned in passing is that of Nigel Tufnel. Guitar slingers from Bernie Weinstock to Russ Cairo have all acknowledged the highly temperate lead lines that have made Tufnel's six-string excursions among the most basic in rock: simplistic without being simple. Yet among the fans who find themselves enthralled with Tufnel's stage presence and endearing looks, there is perhaps not enough recognition of his skills as an *axeman* to separate him from the pack of other-than-competent guitarists. Which brings up the very question of the man's identity, apart from his obvious status as lead guitarist of Spinal Tap.

Who is Nigel Tufnel? That's a good question, and maybe it depends on who's doing the asking. Nige—his mates call him that so frequently I feel justified in using the sobriquet (look it up, sucker!) myself—Nige seems so affable, so accessible onstage and in his public utterances, that the average fan may be surprised to discover that he is not among the easiest people in the world to interview. Even for a seasoned reporter like yours truly, one approaches the Tufnel persona not without a certain trepidation, based on past experience. Like the time ol' Nige sat through an interview crunching away on a Granny Smith apple and muttering his replies in such an unintelligible fashion that halfway along I snapped off my tape recorder and left.

Recently I caught Tufnel in a more receptive mood, following Spinal Tap's triumphant six-city farewell tour of America. All he was chewing on was his beloved gum, and I was able to get down to brass tacks on a number of guitar-related topics with the man who has made "11" a household number.

HIT STREAM: When did you first start playing guitar?
NIGEL TUFNEL: That really is up for grabs. Because my memory has taken quite a nose dive, and the doctors have said it's partially from playing loud for so long—and partly they say "Just genes," whatever that's supposed to mean. But I think I was about four when I first was attracted to music, and probably around seven when I got my first guitar, which was called a Big Ben. It was actually a very *little* guitar, and a cheap one—it was something like ten shillings. My dad got it for me.

HS: Do you remember why you started?
NT: I was hearing music on the radio all the time. A lot of American blues records were being played and I thought, well, I'd

jump on the bandwagon, so to speak.

HS: What were some of your earliest influences?
NT: Jimmy the Spot . . . I never knew his real last name, but he grew up in Squatney. I was about four or five years old and he was already quite an accomplished skiffle player, y'know, and he was great. He really encouraged me to play loud. He said, "What 'ave you got to be ashamed of?" And I said, "Nothing," and he said, "Well, then let everyone *hear* it." And more than that, even. So it was pretty much the beginnings of my volume obsession, I s'pose.

HS: Where is Squatney, by the way?
NT: East End of London.

HS: It's hard to find it on maps, for some reason.
NT: Yeah, well, you know for a while they took it *off* the map. 'Cause they were so ashamed—it was *not* a great tourist area, and they figured, y'know, people who *lived* there knew where it was, so why put it on the map?

HS: How did that make *you* feel, as a native?
NT: Well, I didn't have a map, so I didn't know any of this was going on to begin with. I just heard about this years later, so I don't care, really.

HS: Did you have any formal musical training?
NT: Not formal like conservatory or anything like that. I can't read music; I can read chord symbols, but no formal training, no.

HS: You're well known as a guitar collector and fancier. What's your main squeeze, guitar-wise?

NT: My main guitar has been for quite a while a Gibson gold-top Les Paul from 1955 with stock pickups; it's got what they call T-90 pickups. And I use GHS Boomer strings, "nines" they're called, extra-light gauge. And that's my main guitar. I have many other guitars, fifty or sixty guitars, but I record with that guitar and I take it on the road even though I have to protect it because it's quite valuable.

HS: Ever had any trouble with people trying to boost it?
NT: No. I've had trouble tuning it, though. In San Francisco I went through a whole first set really quite out of tune. I don't know if it's me; maybe it's that deafness setting in.

HS: Of all your collectibles, do you have a favorite?
NT: I've got some *rare* guitars, some one-of-a-kind. I have a Kafinetti. It has thirteen pickups on it—it has a humbucker pickup, it has ten single-coil pickups, and it's got two what-do-you-call-it, jazz sort of pickups. It's got about forty-five dials on it and it's a great-sounding guitar. I use it once in a while. It's a double cutaway. It was made for me by an old chap over in Rome. It's rare—it's worth maybe twenty thousand in your money.

HS: Kind of the Stradivarius of guitars, eh?
NT: Well . . . no. It's a guitar, it's not a violin.

HS: What do you consider to be your finest moment on record?
NT: I suppose—I don't know if it was released over here, but we did this live show at Whimpton, with David and I doing I think it was about a two-hour solo back and forth. It was a jazz-blues festival, this was early Seven-

ties, I s'pose, and it's hard to get over here; they've got an import.

HS: Was that *Silent But Deadly*?
NT: Could've been. Song was called "Short 'n' Sweet," "Short 'n' Easy"—don't remember really, it was so long ago. I remember in my mind that what we were playin' was great.

HS: And it was just an ol' blues improv?
NT: Yeah. Y'know, everything, all rock 'n' roll, no matter what anyone says, is really just fancy blues. It's all basics, and if you really look at it, it's all the same, y'know? It's nothing new, really. And of course the old blues that came from Chicago and Mississippi and all, New Orleans—you trace that back 'cross the Atlantic to Africa. And then from Africa it goes back to, I guess, uh, Belgium.

HS: Belgium?
NT: Yes, where, really, the very roots of that blues form take place, y'know. And then Holland, of course, is the real, is the main place. That's why when we were playing with Jan Van Der Kvelk, when we were the Dutchmen, he had such a natural way of playin', and I did some research and really found out that, y'know, all those people in the sixteenth century were really startin', y'know, to play good slide guitar. And they would sit on those what they call the canal things there—y'know, those dykes—and they would break an old bottle of Heineken or whatever they were drinkin' and just slide up the guitar.

HS: How many hours a day do you practice?
NT: I don't really have time much anymore for practicin'. I play but I don't practice. It's dif-

ferent—I don't sit and play scales. It's too boring, and I can't play them anyway. So what I do is I fuck about. Y'know, that's more fun, just fuckin' about. But I recommend for younger children to practice. You've got to play as much as you can: as much as you can, as loud as you can. That's the rule; that's the Tufnel motto.

HS: I like that; it's got a nice ring to it.
NT: Thank you.

HS: Your fans would probably like another live album. Any plans?
NT: Well, we talk; but nothing firm right now. 'Cause we do take a vote; we each have an equal vote, except for Richard Shrimpton, Mick's twin brother, and Viv [Savage]—they have half-votes. But we vote, and we don't have a majority yet that would say yes to a live record at this time. Although, y'know, my solo project, which I'm working on, is really shaping up quite nicely.

HS: You've got another solo project?
NT: Yeah, I'm doing one of those home recordings. I've got one of those home recording studios and I'm doing a lot of overdubbing. I'm playing all the instruments, doing all the vocals, even playing the drums. It's Moses' flight from Egypt, in, y'know, a suite. Right now it's called "Pyramid Blues," and it's in the form of a sort of blues, y'know: Woke up this morning, It was too hot. . . .Get me out of this desert, y'know, I'm tired of lookin' at these wedges.

HS: Your first solo project, *Nigel Tufnel's Clam Caravan*, was never released here in the States, and I wonder if you could tell us something about it.

NT: That was a rather grandiose sort of project. It was also in the form of a suite, but using large orchestration sort of technique —which I find now, in my older age, to be just a ruse, really. Y'know, you hear all these Beethoven records with hundred-piece orchestras—it's only an excuse to play loud, y'know. Otherwise, why wouldn't they just use *one* violin, *one* trumpet, *one* bass, *one* clarinet? I just think he went overboard. They didn't have electronics then, so what they did was just add musicians and play louder.

HS: But what is the significance of *Clam Caravan*?
NT: The title? Well, some of these things are lost in translation and can't really be explained. The Chinese say . . . What do the Chinese eat with?

HS: Chopsticks?
NT: Right. So what's that supposed to mean? Or what the Spanish people use to make that clicking sound.

HS: Castanets.
NT: Yeah, see? There you go again.

HS: But didn't it have a significance to *you*?
NT: Oh, I see what you mean. Yeah, it probably did at the time, but, y'know, the waves of history have long since covered it over, I guess.

HS: Not to mention drugs and drink.
NT: Oh, no. I don't really like to dwell on that. My drug days are over, and I've found a new way of approaching my craft without the use of drugs.

HS: What's that?
NT: Well, it's drinking, mostly.

. . .But even that is not really done to a large extent anymore. I'm just too fucking old, really. I mean, I have a drink at night, a drink in the morning, and that's it.

HS: Has near-success changed your life-style?
NT: You get phone calls late at night; you get birds waiting in the hotel lobby, y'know; you get sent strange undergarments; you get the usual sort of screaming people once in a while, yeah. For a while I had a bodyguard.

HS: What was his name?
NT: His name was Leo Weiss. He was a nice chap, about five foot eight, balding. . . .

HS: Doesn't sound like much of a bodyguard.
NT: Well, I didn't know that at the time. He ended up embezzling about twenty thousand pounds from Tap, Inc., actually. But he told me he was a bodyguard, and I took him at his word.

HS: Could you explain a technique you use in your soloing that might help our readers when they play guitar?
NT: I've got a certain technique that no one else really uses. In "Heavy Duty," I do a free-form beginning, which is a blues in A, and I've found that the frets on the guitar have a numerological significance. The third fret, where you play G on the E string —so you go A-B-C-D-E-F-G is seven, and three is ten, minus five is five, and five is my lucky number. And, y'know, solos, great solos, start like that many times.

HS: So your advice to our guitar-playing readers would be what?
NT: Pick your lucky day. My lucky day, July second. July— January, February, March . . .

seven, right? And two: nine. Minus four: five, my lucky number. So you got your lucky day, your lucky number. So you add those up and you move around the frets a bit and you find a solo from it. Quite simple.

HS: Are you particular about what you wear onstage these days?
NT: I used to wear a lot of these tight clothes, these Spandex sort of trousers. Now I wear black jeans and sneaks so you can run about, a tight shirt that shows my muscles. But I don't wear those tight trousers—one reason was, if you're havin' a pee before you go on, it leaves a bit of an annoying spot right in front. And everyone in the front row says, "Lookit that spot." An' it gets bigger; then there's sort of this ever-widening circle. And there's nothing you can do when you're up there playing; you can't get out a blow dryer and *blow* it. So I figured, Wear jeans and a regular pair of underwear, and, y'know, don't even be bothered with all this sexual sort of thing anymore. . . . I mean, I *will* drop my trousers once in a while if we're really playing hot and there seems to be a cute bird in the front row; I'll give her a little look at the little gent with the fire hat once in a while.

HS: Is it particularly difficult to sing and play guitar at the same time, which you are sometimes called upon to do?
NT: No, only if I'm playing in D. There's some mental block I have against singing and playing in D. I don't know what it is, but usually, if we're doing a song in D, I just don't sing.

HS: What do you think about when you're playing a solo? You have that look of intense concen-tration, maybe even pain, on your face. What's going on?
NT: Well . . . lots of times it *is* pain, because the high E string gets caught underneath your nail. And sometimes I think about my girlfriend, Regina Chud.

HS: What's it like playing with David St. Hubbins, and how do you know when it's your turn to solo?
NT: It's great playin' with him; we've been plain together for twenty years or somethin', and we really have the same brain. You've heard about that movie, *The Man with Two Brains*—well, this isn't like that, it's like two people with one brain: *The Two Men with One Brain*. Sharing the brain. And as to when we know, we don't—you can only listen. If he starts to play and we're both playing at the same time, we sort of look at each other for a while like, One of us better drop out. And then we do.

HS: Do you employ backward masking on your records?
NT: I think on "Devil" we did it, but we sort of signed a pact. I'm not really allowed to divulge what that was. But as a general principle, I don't think it's a good idea, it takes too much studio time.

HS: But it only takes a few minutes.
NT: Well, not the way *we* do it. We phonetically figure out what we're doing and try to sing backward.

HS: Why not just overdub a tape going backward like other heavy-metal groups?
NT: Well, we didn't know that. We found out much later, but then it was too late, we'd spent about six hours of studio time doin' that.

HS: If you *could* use backward masking cheaply, what message would you like to send?
NT: I think, Get enough sleep; do *some* exercise, if not every day then every *other* day, and, uh, y'know, just have fun.

HS: At the end of "Heavy Duty" there appears to be a classical music riff and I was wondering if you could identify it and tell us whose idea it was.
NT: It was my idea. It's sort of a tribute to the classical masters of bygone eras, of old dead people with wigs. It sort of covers the whole generation from Mozart to Bach to Beethoven. Those three are my influences, really.

HS: How did they influence you?
NT: Well, Beethoven was deaf, which is the direction *I'm* going in, so I can relate to *that*. Mozart, they just made a movie about him, and he was thirty-five when he died—and I'm older than that, so I feel lucky about that. And Bach, y'know, he just had all these children, so he must've been, y'know, dippin' the oil stick quite a bit, so I can really sort of relate to all of 'em really.

HS: But musically what impressed you?
NT: Well, Bach just wrote all this filigree sort of music using these trumpets and violins and everything. He just, y'know, kept doing it—and I guess I admire his stick-to-itiveness.

HS: Any chance of "Christmas with the Devil" being released as a seasonal single this December?
NT: We're trying. We're doin' our best. It's not shapin' up. The earliest commitment we had was end of February.

HS: That would sort of miss the

seasonal market, wouldn't it?
NT: Well, yeah; but if you look at it the other way, the other offer we had was, uh, June. So at least it'll be cold out, that's the way I look at it. It's really the lesser of two evils, if you'll pardon the expression.

HS: What about guitar picks—any favorites?
NT: I use two different types for different tunes. I use Tortex, the yellow ones; and I use Fender medium. Those two get me through everything.

HS: Ever use any custom-made picks?
NT: Yes, for a while in the early days when I was playing mostly blues, I had them made from macadamia-nut shells. They would be made in Hawaii for me, sent over in these little packages—handmade macadamia nut plectrums. And, y'know, the nuts were not *in* them, it was just from the shells. They would last two or three months each pick. But then, of course, it just got to be too much of a pain to send for that little package, so I just went to the plastic.

HS: How would you characterize the musical style of Tap around the time of *Nerve Damage, Brainhammer,* and *Blood to Let*? After your "psychedelic" period but before the "art rock" or "concept" era of *Rock and Roll Creation* and *The Sun Never Sweats,* or the late-glam *Bent for the Rent*?
NT: Well, y'know, it's pre-glam, is what it is. But other than that, I wouldn't really know how to put my finger on pigeonholing it. I would say it was the Forgotten Rock 'n' Roll, period. Leave it at that.

HS: Do you ever consider the longevity of Spinal Tap?
NT: How do you mean?

HS: Well, do you ever look back and say, "Gosh, how did we ever survive all these years and—"
NT: Well, I never say "Gosh." I don't use that word.

HS: What would you say, then?
NT: I'd say, Cor . . . if we've survived up till now, let's keep pluggin' along. I don't like to think of myself as being anything unusual, other than a *pioneer.* You've got to acknowledge that, though; you've got to face reality, y'know. Which is only saying to people, as my friend Jimmy the Spot said to me, "Turn it up—what have you got to be ashamed of?"

HS: How do you feel about rock videos? Having just released your very first, "Hell Hole"?
NT: Can't really make heads or tails of it, really. Seems amusin' up to a point, and not that amusin' after that. And I can't really follow a lot of the stories on them. I don't have MTV, I only have those radios that get TV sound, so I can't really figure out . . .

HS: Could you give us your preference in amps?
NT: Well, I normally use Marshall stacks, and you've got to be very careful because either they're very good or they're very bad. I've been working with some custom companies, though, that come to me with super amplification units, because I need even more punch than the Marshalls can provide. And there is talk about making available to the public amps that go up to eleven—and, of course, my guitars now go up to eleven as well. So that makes twenty-two, which is a great number. Two is February, and two is like July second, which is my lucky day. And you add three, it's five: my lucky number. Comes back to that.

HS: What are your immediate plans after the big tour?
NT: Just laying low for a while. Trying to get into some of this Hungarian music. It's crazy stuff, really nuts: They play fast, then they play slow, then they get all wiggly. I'm thinking of doing some world sort of trips to just get soaked in the atmosphere of music of other nations. I'm thinking of going to, y'know, Canada.

Taken from *Hit Stream,* May 1982

MY TOP TEN

(Photo by Karen Murphy)

DAVID ST. HUBBINS
Spinal Tap

1. DION: Ruby Baby That was the moment that loose rock 'n' roll vocalizing was born. Everything relaxed a bit and you didn't have to be all that tensed up to sing—a great moment in casual rock!

2. NANCY SINATRA: How Does That Grab You Darlin'? The follow-up to the much inferior "These Boots Are Made for Walkin'." A much better work, the other end of the spectrum from Dion, and just a great vocal performance.

3. DONOVAN: The Trip Mainly because it was the only song that really fully re-created an actual psychedelic experience. It felt like you were there—or at least invited and had to turn it down, but still wanted to be there. It was just an extremely magnetic recording for me.

4. JOHN D. LOUDERMILK: Road Hog A fairly obscure disc by the author of "Teen Angel"— you know, the one where the bloke takes her out in the car and she gets crushed by a train or something. No one gets killed in this, but there's still cars and it's a novelty record.

5. THE ROBINS: Cherry Lips A classic R&B performance—the Robins later became the Coasters, y'know. I'm not sure what label it was on originally, because I have it on a compilation of recordings by smaller labels that were then bought up by large labels that were then bought up by the Cosa Nostra, and they released 'em privately. So it's a bit difficult to track down.

6. THE THIRD RAIL: Run Run Run Real uptempo stuff by a late-Sixties garage band from New York, I believe.

MY TOP TEN
DEREK SMALLS
Spinal Tap

1. JOHN FRED & THE PLAY-BOY BAND: Judy in Disguise with Glasses

2. THE SOUL SURVIVORS: Expressway to Your Heart

3. GORDON LIGHTFOOT: Canadian Railroad Trilogy You'll find the common denominator in most of these is just a dynamite bass part that just sort of sets the song off. I don't know if you remember "Judy in Disguise" went doo-doodoo dum doo-doot, duh-doot, doodoo-doo doom—just a great, great, great, great bass part that goes all the way through it. And "Expressway to Your Heart": dum, dum, duhduhdum buh*duh* boom—remember that?

4. THE AMERICAN BREED: Bend Me Shape Me There again, same thing: great, classic bass part.

5. DAVE CLARK 5: Catch Us If You Can Just 'cause of the drone . . . from *Havin' a Wild Weekend.* They blew it, though—they really blew it, man. I just think they had a chance to be the Beatles and they blew it. They didn't push it. Personally, I blame Dave, but I don't know that

much about the workings of the group, so . . .

6. SYMARYP: Skinhead Moonstomp One of the old ska classics. I keep tellin' the boys we should do a dub mix of some of this stuff. I bet it *would* work with heavy metal, too! You get some of those eeeeerieee effects . . . just imagine what a dub mix of "Rock and Roll Creation" would sound like.

7. DONOVAN: Legend of the Girl-Child Linda That's a private thing, though. That's not for any of the reasons that you might expect. Let's just say that reminds me of the best mushroom trip I ever had in my life, so I have to put that on. I never had the

7. THE JIVE FIVE: My True Story A great mellow moment in rock.

8. THE BILL BLACK COMBO: White Silver Sands Bill Black, of course, became, if not famous, then certainly—well, not even near-famous, he became near the famous, I guess is the way you'd say it. Near-the-famous Bill Black, because he was near a very famous person; but this one he did on his own—it's a great record.

9. THE BROTHERS FOUR: Greenfields A great ballad, which was from the motion picture *The Alamo*—which I did remember seein' when I was on the road in Amsterdam. That was back when we were working with Jan Van Der Kvelk . . . we saw it in Dutch—no, we saw it in English with Dutch subtitles. All I recall was it was very exciting and the song was the same. It's always had a very deep sort of meaning for me, because I do identify with the Americans in that film.

At the time I was living in a very small building, it was very crowded, and I felt oftentimes the wish that I had a gun. I don't know exactly—I mean that bloke John Wayne, he gets stabbed through the gut and the thing breaks off in the door in back of him and there's blood all over the place— he's still fightin'!

I like to think of myself in that way. You got a guitar; you know, it's better than a gun, really, because no one can really kill you. But I just admired him in that film. I'm a big John Wayne fan.

10. THE CLASSICS FOUR: Spooky I think that's a great boppin' little song.

11. LITTLE PEGGY MARCH: I Will Follow Him I think that's a great song, mostly because I knew that she was young and she was short, and yet she made this great big, noisy record. It occurs to me that most of these are American records—in fact, all of them are, with the possible exception of "The Trip," but where I'm stayin' here this bloke has a lot of American records and that's what I'm sort of looking through.

I do sort of hate to see my own people underrepresented on this list. But I think what it was is that I didn't really listen to a lot of my contemporaries when I was playin'. I mean, these days I've had a little bit more time to actually sit and listen. It's great—I've become a sort of like gray eminence; I can just sit about and listen to . . . and some of it was, y'know, *garbage*, and I was amazed to find out that it was enormously successful. But what are you going to do?

From *Maxi Hits*, May 1981

chance to ask him, but I feel certain that he was on mushrooms when he did that.

8. TONY WILSON: The Big Hurt First record to use phasing. It was like they were on acid in 1957. I mean, they were doing experiments with it back then, so it's not impossible.

9. TOM JONES: It's Not Unusual Just for pure, pure pizzazz. Just for pure getting pizzazz into the grooves—because we are all showmen. That's something I learned with Skaface. If you notice, it's always called a Jamaican *show*band, because we were not primarily a music band. We prided ourselves on doing the fastest-moving fifty-five minutes in Britain at the time. It was just constant motion: dipping and sliding and all those moves. It was a great school for me. Much more time spent rehearsing the moves than the music, *much* more. And it showed. So even though people say, "Tom Jones, get off it!" there is a showmanship that comes through the grooves of that record that I perceive even if no one else does.

10. LULU: To Sir with Love I never saw the movie—I never heard the record, I'm just nominating it. No, just kidding. It's not my favorite record, it just came to mind. Lulu's still very big over there; she has that soulful catch in her voice that's *quite* interesting. . . . No, I would say, let me change my ten.

10. THE FANTASTIC JOHNNY C: Boogaloo Down Broadway Again for the bass part, which is so killer in that. Then they'll just say Derek doesn't like women, because I didn't nominate any, but that's OK. The proof is obvious.

From *Maxi Hits*, April 1980

MY TOP TEN

NIGEL TUFNEL
Spinal Tap

1. JIMMY ALFANO: Green, Green, Green The greatest. Just the greatest, everyone knows why he's the greatest. He's just great—the greatest.

2. THE WEAVERS: The Weavers at Carnegie Hall I just like the sound, really; I don't like the music itself. I like the engineering on that one—just put "great engineering." The songs are quite stupid.

3. SOUND EFFECTS: Sound Effects No. 6 That's the one with the motor raceways, "Famous Raceways." Daytona's my favorite, it's not even close. Watkins Glen is almost up there, but I'd say Daytona for sheer downshifting. I mean, in stereo it's just fabulous.

4. LESLEY GORE: It's My Party Just put A-plus. She was poppin' out of a cake or something on the British cover, but the American version was probably different.

5. JAN PEERCE: My Holiday Favorites He was a rabbi—a cantor, they call it. He wasn't *actually* a rabbi, though.

6.–10. Use your imagination. That really thins it out, you see. After that, you're really getting into desperation territory. I just say use your imagination from six to ten, that's what I'd say.

Q: You mean I should just make it up when I publish this?
A: No, don't make it up; just say, "Use your imagination." Didn't mean for *you* to use your imagination. God forbid!

From *Maxi Hits,* January 1981

WISE UP

Got a question about just almost anyone or anything to do with Spinal Tap? Well, stuff it! No, seriously, just send it in and our Muggsy will get you the answer.

I've been having an argument with my friend about where Spinal Tap got their name from (from whence?). I say it comes from a line in the Beatles song "Come Together" ("He got Ono sideboard/He one spinal tapper"); she says they got it from a medical-supply catalog. Who's right?
Julie Stickle, Wantaugh, New York.

• Neither of you wins this one, I'm afraid, although careful consultation with the members of Tap has yielded equally confusing answers. According to David, "It's an anagram of a Dutch beer, though not one of us can recall the name." Not surprising, that, since when queried Nigel insisted that "I just thought of it one day. It's just a name." And Derek, who had the most compelling answer, rambled on at rather too much length for our purposes. Essentially his explanation went like this: "We were fetching about for a name that conveyed images of power and pain. Obviously, if you're getting a spinal tap, someone's in power over *you*, see. That was the image we were trying to convey: power-dominance-pain as an experience of musical beauty. And I believe it was Nigel's uncle had just had one, so that brought it to mind." Odd how that fact had escaped Nigel's memory, but I suppose we shouldn't be surprised.

In the lyrics to "Sex Farm" that were reprinted in the July issue of *Spinal Vibes*, the following lines appear: "Sex farm woman/ Don't you see my sallow eyes/I-I-I'm/Working on a sex farm." My question is this—Why would Tap use a line like "sallow eyes"? I mean, it sounds so literary and all that. Please explain.
Debra Bartlett, Dover, Delaware

• Whoops, are our cheeks red! Looks like we goofed. The line should read: "Don't you see my silo rising high" ("and that's fairly literary itself," adds David). Derek explains: "'Silo rising,' you see. Farm—it's a farm image: where you store your wheat. But I've seen it reprinted wrong in thousands of places [!] and I've said to David, 'Maybe you should sing it more clearly.' And he's said, 'I sing it plenty clearly, thank you,' and then we get into one of *those*." We here at *Spinal Vibes* sure know all about *those!*

I really love Spinal Tap, especially that foxy Nigel Tufnel. Can you please tell me some personal information about him, such as his birthday, color of eyes, early life, marital status, etc. Also, is he married or does he have a girlfriend or both?
Dolores Contini, Ramsey, New Jersey

• We'll let Nigel tackle this one, personally.
"Thank you very much. I'd be glad to. Color of eyes: green. Early life: enjoyable. Marital status: single. Not married, no girlfriend."

My dad says he is an old Tap fan from the hippie days (disgusting, eh?), and even remembers seeing the band on "Jamboree-bop" on telly back in 1968 (that was before Woodstock!). He also recalls the B-side of their first single as Tap, a song called "Rainy Day Sun," which was never released on LP. (He describes it as a cross between Dylan and Henrix—can that possibly be?) I'd like to know if you know anyone who would know where I could find a copy. I'm an avid collector of Spinal Tap. Thanks a bunch.
Peter McMaster, Ratho Station, Midlothian, Scotland

• As far as I know, the track is available only on either of two import compilations, a Filipino bootleg LP called *Top Hit for Nows* (PUIT-PU702, 1968) and a Japanese album the title of which translates approximately as *Maximum Tap*, on the Japanese Mango label (no relation to the Island Records subsidiary). The song was never available on LP in America or England. Says Nigel, "It's not my favorite tune, to be quite honest. I think it's a bit soft, a bit silly, and I couldn't recommend anyone finding it. I don't have a copy myself. And I'd say it was closer to Dave Weddeck—he's a Welsh rock 'n' roller but you never heard of him, probably. He used to sing with Sissy Cargill down in Swansea. Just sort of country whimsy, not very heavy stuff."

Derek wonders wistfully if he'll ever get the credit he's due.

My mom wonders if Derek Smalls of Tap is the same Derek Smalls who played bass for the all-white Jamaican showband Skaface in the mid-Sixties. He is not credited on a Skaface track that appears on *Still More Intensified! Original Ska 1964–68 (The White Years).* **Also, are any other Skaface records available?**
Rose Ashton, Patagonia, Arizona

• "Yes, that's our Derek," said David St. Hubbins when reached by phone at his new southern California villa. (Seems Dave has become quite Americanized since Tap's recent tour!) He added, "Apparently, the intensifying process did not include *research*." I did a little, however,

and came up with one other compilation, *Saturday Night in Toxtoth*, that features a couple of Skaface cuts—"Jam It Up" and "Jam It Up (Part 2)." Again, Smalls is not credited, but as Derek himself points out, this was before the era where the names of all the sidemen appeared on album jackets. "You look at those Motown records and try to find out who played bass or guitar on a particular cut, you can't do it. It was like a different ethic, y'know? 'Fuck the musician' was the ethic in those days. Thank God we've lived through to better times.

"But again, because the music was not really the important thing, it was hard to capture what was great about Skaface on record—at least most record-company people thought so. No Skaface album exists or ever existed. There was a bootleg that came out years later of one of our shows—I was amazed to see that someone had gone to this much trouble, because they had made a proper cover and everything—called *Can't Stop Sitting*. That's because people sat to watch us because we were such a show. We made one appearance on Swedish TV, they came over and shot us. 'Rockskjevag' was the name of the show, so anybody who might have a tape of that would have ahold of something mighty precious today, lemme tell you—a Skaface video.

"My hair was cut very short then. I was going for the look of a black man who was trying to straighten his hair to *look* white—but I *was* white, so I had it to begin with, which made it even more difficult. I had to *make* it look like I'd gone through caustic chemicals to get my hair straight when in fact it was just straight. It's the tail of the dog that binds."

"There *were* a few other white ska bands, but not many. Lemme see . . . Jammin' Jimmy Jefferson and the Jesters—a name that was catchy without being memorable—was a white band that played up north for a while; they were out of Manchester. Now I don't know if it was their attitude or what, but they got beat up a lot at the venues, which *we* avoided somehow. I think we just had more of a good-time image, somehow, but they were a bit more aggressive about being white. It was not a popular form for white musicians to go into at the time."

I have been following the accounts in the papers of those Long Island Satanists who tortured their victim and gouged his eyes out before killing him. They testified that they listened to AC/DC records during the sacrificial ceremony. How would members of Tap feel, I wonder, had it been *their* **records serving as the sound track to slaughter —as it might well have been?**
Jim Checkley, New England, North Dakota

• Since this is obviously a touchy subject, I think it's best just to let DD&N have their own say.
NIGEL: Well, it's a hypothetical question, isn't it? I mean, how would you feel if your father had shot J.R.? What am I supposed to say? I can't react to a question based on fiction. I don't think our fans do that. Maybe some lesser heavy metal groups have that effect, but I like to think our fans wouldn't do that.
DEREK: You try to control every element of what you do. It's hard enough to control what the record company does with your work, as you know from our history. Once it passes out of your hands into the stream of

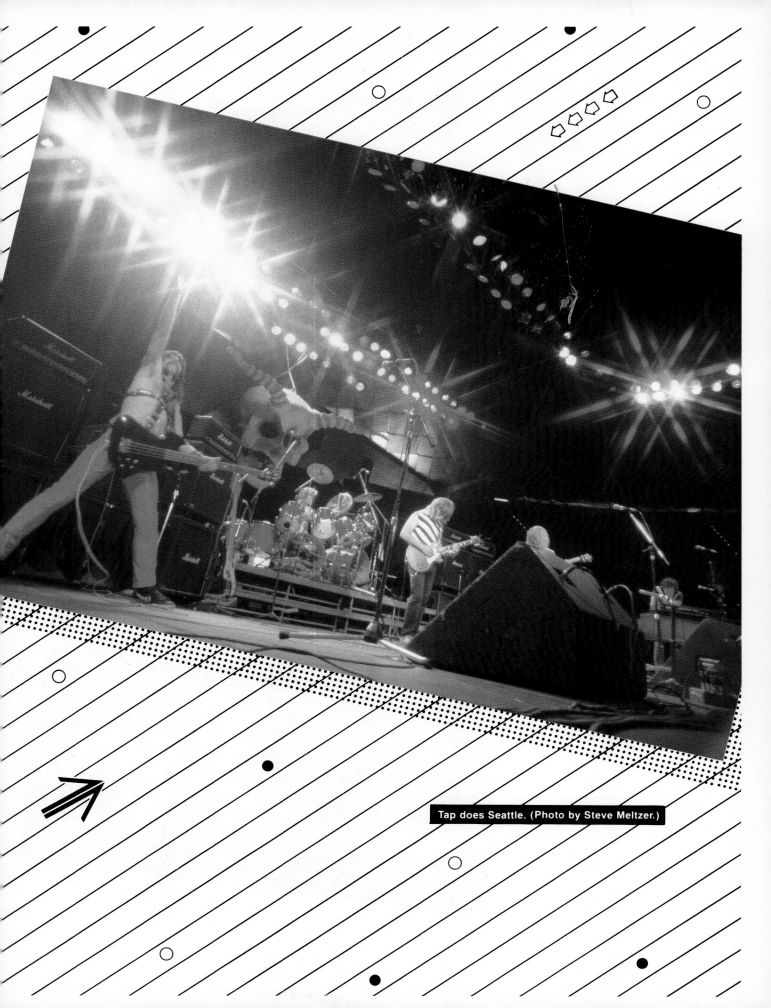

Tap does Seattle. (Photo by Steve Meltzer.)

(Collection of the author.)

Live from New York, it's Spinal Tap. (Collection of the author.)

(Photos by Steve Meltzer.)

"I'll drink to that!"—The End of an Era.
(Photo by Steve Meltzer.)

Nigel, kilts and all, at the entrance to his castle (somewhere in Scotland) as he appeared in *Fodor's Guide to Scotland.* During the band's collective dark night of the soul, they spent much of their time here.

Tap's historic signing with Polymer Records. *Right to left:* Tufnel, St. Hubbins, Ric Shrimpton (Mick's younger brother), Viv Savage, tour manager Ian Faith, and (seated) Sir Denis Eton-Hogg, Smalls.

Knocking on heaven's door.

On the set of the ''Hell Hole'' video.

commerce, then it belongs to them. That's the record company's attitude and the attitude of the fans. I would be proud to have our records played anywhere at any time, as part of any ceremony, because that means that we mean something to someone. The writer says this was a brutal ceremony—but then, it's a brutal world, innit? What if our records were played during a slaughtering of cattle? I would be proud, because it would be saying that men who are at hard, brutal work choose our music to give them a bit of light and inspiration and cheer. So there you go. And it might be helping the cattle along on their road to an untimely demise.

The stereotype view is that listening to this music inspires them to kill. Maybe listening to this music would make them kill one person less. Maybe they'll stop sooner—who knows? It's not science, is it? It's all hunches. Maybe this was the music that helped the victims feel better before the end. Let's put it *this* way: If *you* were the victim of a ritual slaughter, wouldn't you wanna go out listening to decent music, given the choice? Given the choice, of course, you'd rather not be the victim of ritual slaughter. But if *that* choice is taken from you, you'd rather listen to decent music during the event. I mean, they could've put on *Metal Machine Music* or somethin'. It's all relative. It seems so simple, so cut-and-dried—cut-and-dried, I don't mean that, but . . .

DAVID: As long as they weren't involved in home taping, it's really not our lookout.

Well, thanks guys, and a copy of Lou Reed's classic *Metal Machine Music* is on its way to North Dakota.

Some of the last Tap T-shirts on sale in America (Seattle, to be exact), but not a ''CANCELLED'' stencil in sight. (Photo by H. Shearer.)

Could you please tell me where I could get hold of a Spinal Tap "Tap Into America" tour T-shirt with the "CANCELLED" stencil on the back, without having to enter a competition? I'm desperate to complete my collection of Tapiana.
Derek's Moustache, Barking, Essex, England

• I'm sorry, but your very desperation makes you a competitor. What's more, you've lost. Try again. We certainly don't have any free T-shirts here in the *Spinal Vibes* office, but—wait . . . seems Derek himself has an idea. *(Will wonders never cease?—Ed.)* "I would say you would have to fuck someone in the record company to get one of those nowadays. That was a special shirt that was put out just sort of to rub our noses in it, 'cause relations with Polymer were not too good, if you remember. Ian [Faith, Tap manager] has had most of those T-shirts destroyed. They are, in fact, worth more than the records these days, more in some cases than the concert tickets themselves. But it's just collector-mania, it has nothing to do with people who are really into the music. It's like those people who were trading pins at the Olympics that never *watched* the Olympics—experience is substi-

tuted for by the memento of the experience itself, so where are you at then?"

What do Spinal Tap think, I would like to know, of the accusations appearing in recent issues of *Kerrang* and *Kick Ass* magazines that they are representatives of "False Metal," not worthy to share the same stage with the likes of Slayer, Metallica, Venom, Hellhammer, Anthrax and other genuine metallers?
Dave Humphries, San Diego, California

• Judging from their reactions, they don't much care for the notion. Nigel told me he thinks "it's a pile, a huge pile. That's my answer. Of course I defend us. It's a ridiculous question, a joke question, it's a joke." And are they true metallers or not? "True. True to the bone." Derek feels that the question is looking at metal "as a cult, as a small insular world. We've never felt metal was like that: 'Yes, *you* can get in; no, *you can't* get in.' First of all, we don't call ourselves 'heavy metal,' for starters. We call ourselves 'light-to-medium metal' because we can do so many other things. I think we've been all along a band with a broader vision, to be truthful, and you get it from both sides then. Your art rockers say, 'Well, they're not real art rockers,' and the metalheads will say, 'Yeah, they're not real metalheads.' But the rest of the people, we're sayin' something to them: Come along, we're not a cult. We're bigger than and smaller than a cult."

David, taking the whole thing a bit more lightly, adds, "We might say this in answer: If we're *false* metal, why do we get so rusty?"

(Though it's unrelated to the original question, I couldn't help asking Derek how ST could be

David and Nigel model those carefully combed coiffures—and how about those cod-pieces, ladies?

both bigger *and* smaller than a cult. His answer is, I think, fascinating: "We're bigger in that the *idea* is bigger; in terms of records sold, though . . . It works both ways, dunnit? That's that yin-yang thing again, rears its ugly head again. Y'know, David and Nigel, the dark one and the light one. It rears it so often in our lives, we've been obsessed by it. Each of us takes turns—that's what I think the secret of the group is. That each of us takes turns being in different ways the Mr. Yin for a moment, and then someone else will be Mr. Yang and then it switches around. So no one ever gets boxed in by being total yin, 'cause that'd be a drag after a while.")

Being great fans of Spinal Tap's music and looks, my brother and I would like to know the name of both David and Nigel's hairdressers and all the relevant details. Also, how would they describe their hairstyles?
Ruby Weingarten, Rhinebeck, New York
• Says Nigel, "Well, my hairdresser's name is Nigel Tufnel. And I wouldn't describe it any way except it's just me." And, keeping it all in the family, David claims that "Jeanine does mine at the same time her brother Julian does hers. It's *Cosmic!*"
  Indeed.

From *Spinal Vibes*—the only official Spinal Tap fanzine—various issues.

Star★Flap

Spinal Tap's
DAVID ST. HUBBINS

"It's great staying in southern California right now—I really like this part of the country. You know, the Olympics were here up until just days ago. I didn't go to any actual events, but it was wonderful—I watched them all on telly. I pulled a bit for G.B., of course, but I had to get carried away by this American sweep; I thought it was very exciting. I really admired the way they pulled together in time of great divisiveness in the country.

The boycott? Well, you know we were at the 1980 Olympics so I don't feel it's really my right to name names. Actually, we *supported* the American boycott, you know—as much as you can without totally blowing *your* fun. That's support, anyway, in spirit. But I think, Leave politics out of it actually, don't you?"

"I get a lot of questions about Jeanine, but she's my wife now. We've actually had the graft done, a golden ring on my left hand, or at least one finger of it; she's got a similar device and that's that. We're probably gonna put down roots here in southern California —there's something about this place. For one thing, there's certainly as many English rock 'n' roll personnel living here as there are in London, and that's a consideration.''

"I'm expanding my talents —in fact, I'm working on a screenplay now. You know this film bug's really bitten. I did enjoy being involved in that documentary film even though that wasn't really our work. I'm writing a film about the dietary habits of prehistoric man. I'm even thinking of doing a kind of experimental sound track—not rock per se, but something I'd work out on my own. This chap I'm staying with out here has a synthesizer and a Vocoder and you can really make some unusual types of sounds with them. But after that, I haven't really thought about it.''

(Photos by Steve Meltzer.)

"One of the things I objected to in the documentary, though, was the treatment of Jeanine. I really don't think she came off that well; she certainly didn't come off as the Jeanine I know. It was shocking to both of us, really, because that's *not* her at all. It's not *me*, for that matter; it's not either of us. That's the part of the film that bothered Jeanine the most because it does, amazingly enough, actually appear that she sort of pushed her way into something—and nothing could be further from the truth.

"It was just that there was a crisis on the road and she, thank *God*, was there, because we couldn't have finished that particular tour, we never would've gotten to L.A., one thing after another. I think,

personally, she emerges as a very strong person, which *is* the truth. But that shouldn't be confused with a sort of hardness. Ultimately, the film gives a very incomplete view of her. There's no leavening of her character.''

"I was surprised at the lack of sex in the film myself. Because I know that Nigel—Nige has a good time on the road. I myself, being more like a one-woman man—oh, I enjoy the flirtations and the tease and all that, but when the show's over I'm on to shower and into the sheets. Alone. But Nige, he's a high roller, he's a basher, and I'm amazed that he didn't get more of that into the film. But I guess even he has some decency. I know that I've never seen him actually perform sexual acts in front of a full camera crew. It's usually only ten or twelve of us in the hotel room.''

"Yes, that 'Flower People' bit was real, we certainly did go through a psychedelic period. At least, I guess we did—it's all a bit unclear to me now.... You'll have to understand that when I picture the year 1967 in my head, the "7" is sort of smeared and it just winds up ... I kind of come out of the smear at '71. So it's like a bit of a blur to me.

I do recall certain isolated incidents: I recall having my foot run over by a cab sometime in the late Sixties, things like that. But it's difficult to recount those days; I did perhaps overdo it just a bit. I'm better now—back to the old stout when I can get it, and if not, Budweiser!"

"It's funny. Around the time of 'Flower People,' I had not had any hallucinogenic experiences at all. Except for those that might have resulted from a blow to the head, for example. It wasn't until we came to America, as a matter of fact, and someone gave me something in Boston, Massachusetts, in 1967, and I had no idea what it was. I thought maybe it was like a pep pill, which I'd met with before. Soooo, I woke up wanderin' around the Boston Commons asking everyone if they'd seen my spine.

That was not a good experience, and after that I was a bit leery of it—you should pardon the expression. I wound up doing it a few more times, but LSD really was not my drug. It just wasn't for me, even though the enlightenment I found therein I was able to bring to my experiences with other drugs. It intensified the experience of falling down loaded with other substances. In that sense, LSD was a learning tool."

"As for religion, well, Nigel was with a guru for many years—Baba Ram Dass Boot. I did attend a few sessions with Dass Boot.... It was interesting, it was enlightening even. But Nige was obviously gettin' a lot more out of it than I was because he'd, you know, *paid*, and I was just sort of like *auditing*.

Once again, I don't feel that I truly understood any of that until I met Jeanine back in '77 and she sorted it out. She helped me understand all of it because I *wanted* to understand *all of it*. For years I had been doing a lot of reading, searching for paths, ways, answers, truths, as it were. And years later I was still looking for them. So she came along and said, 'No, no, stupid; *look!*' And she helped me see this *one golden road*. It's really quite simple. I really can't go into it, because it's probably too simple to be ex-plained, if you know what I mean. That kind of incredibly complex simplicity that doesn't translate well into words."

"It really has to do with this simple, basic interaction that *we* have, as perceiving entities, with that which we perceive, which is the rest of the world. And if you achieve a certain balance between those two, well, then you still, y'know, got to worry about payin' the rent and feedin' yourself and all this. But you will have that one major relationship taken care of—between you and every other single living or dead object in the universe. Once you get that little *thing* out of the way, it really frees you up. It gives you a *lot* of spare time."

Reprinted from *Metalhead*, December 1984

A DAY TO FORGET

NIGEL TUFNEL

Each issue we ask a different star musician (well, they think they're stars, anyway—Ed.) to recount a memorable day in his or her life since becoming a top entertainer. Although most of them take to this like pigs to whiskey, some—like Spinal Tap's ace guitarist Nigel Tufnel—don't know where to begin. Fools that we are here at Maxi Hits, *we showed Nigel a sample story by Dee Snider of Twisted Sister recounting his adventures on the ski slopes of Austria. For some reason, he felt compelled to match the tale, and though he'd never been skiing (or to Austria), he came up with the following anecdote.*

" I went to Switzerland—it was after *Brainhammer,* and I went by myself to Switzerland. I thought, I'll just clean up a bit—it was real rough, y'know, we'd done a month of touring or something. And I went to Switzerland to this town called Gstaad—it's this famous resort. And it was not winter so there was no skiing, but I did go on a mountain-climbing trip. No one knew who I was, of course, over there, 'cause it was just a bunch of people and sheep running around—it was Switzerland, y'know; they didn't know what was goin' on—people eatin' chocolate . . .

So I went up to this mountain, very high mountain, and I joined a group, y'know, and we were climbin' all about these mountains. We got to the top of one of these Alp mountains, and there was this avalanche, and the whole party's wiped out, except me and the guide. I had had no sort of mountain-climbing experience at all, either—sort of ironic, you know. Then we went down to the lodge, didn't we? Had some dinner. I had an early night.

Was I upset that they were dead? Well, you'd *think* they were dead, but in an avalanche you can't really tell. You've got all this glacial action happening, and churning snow; you don't know for a fact whether they're dead—they're just not *there* anymore. So it takes some of the pain away, knowing that they might still be alive there. This was of course about thirteen years ago, but . . . there's always a chance, I s'pose.

As for why mountain climbing, you know how it goes. You do so many things in your life and once in a while you go, Look, I really want to take a chance on doing something I've never done; and I felt this might be it, y'know, really test myself. And I did. I was quite successful at it—in the fact that I returned, anyway.

It's not meant to be really amusing, but I didn't have a ski trip to tell you, I've never been skiing, but it was the closest I could come to it. . . .

At Sea World or one of those places, I fell in a tank once. It actually was supposed to be a shark tank, and what I didn't know was that they'd moved the sharks to another one. So I was quite hysterical thrashing about—I mean, really causing a *huge* nuisance, just screaming, y'know, 'Get me the bloody hell out of this, y'know, shark tank!'

I saw these people laughing, and it turns out it was just a giant turtle in there. And of course they don't hurt you, but I didn't know that, you see.

From *Maxi Hits,* February 1985

ROOTS

by Robert Ribbold

Each month *Metälhead* journeys back into the past with a rock and roll celebrity. This month's time traveler is Spinal Tap's Derek Smalls.

"One of the great moments of my youth was the day I got accepted by the LSD, the London School of Design—which basically attracted me because of the initials, of course. But then I decided that maybe I had a career as an art director, so I was an art-direction student for a while. And if it weren't for Ronnie Pudding quitting Spinal Tap when he did, who knows? I might be *designing* record album covers now instead of playing on 'em!"

Derek Smalls pauses a moment and lapses into deep thought in an attempt to recapture some of his earliest pre-Spinal memories, going back to his youth in Nilford-on-Null, England. He admits that many of those blasts from his past are hazy, if not lazy, but after some deep mental backtracking, some memories begin to materialize.

"I'd have to say that my homelife in Nilford was pretty normal," remembers Derek. "I worked with me dad for a while. He had a little van—this was after the mill closed—and he would go 'round sanitizing phones. So I would do that, I would do his route to give him an extra day off.

"I'd come in and say, 'I'm Derek, Mr. Smalls's boy, here to sanitize your phone.' And they'd say, 'You're sure you know how to do it? We don't want germs on the instrument!' I'd say, 'I know, thank you very much, I've been trained by me dad.' But actually, when they weren't lookin', I'd spit in it just to show 'em who's boss."

Derek explains the British phobia about germs and the phone as possibly going back to the war and fears of the Nazis using germ warfare. "It's not the cleanest country in the world, as you may have noticed—and normally you can, y'know, pick your nose and eat a roll and nobody objects. But the phone—I think it's because it's an island. It's small, and germs would multiply quickly; they wouldn't go anywhere, 'cause they don't swim, so they'd stay on the island."

Even with all that helping out at home, though, Derek had time to indulge a more than healthy curiosity in the opposite number.

"My first girlfriend was a very strange woman. She was older than I—I was thirteen, she was fifteen. I met her at school—she was the only exotic dancer in Nilford, which was already very appealing. She would come into the local and do a bit of stripping on a Friday or Saturday night and the boys would get very excited. Because I was a musician, she took a liking to me, she really took me under her wing, as it were. It was a bit of *that*, y'know; it was like, Oooh, yeah, crash course, thank *you*. Her name was Miriam."

"She showed you the ropes, eh?" I ask.

"Well, uh, yeah. First the chains, *then* the ropes, as it were. There *was* a bit of that, as a matter of fact, and it was a bit daunting for me. I said 'Ow!' and she said, 'You don't like *that?* All right, let's try *this.*'"

Derek's initiation into the mysteries of education carried over into his pursuit of even higher education at the London School of Design, where he soon was creating student layouts for adverts that never appeared but which got good marks.

"They said, 'These could be real adverts with a little bit of work,'" smirks Derek. "And I said, 'Well, if I had a little bit of work, I'd *do* real adverts.' But I did an advert for, oh, what was the name of the prophylactic? I forget, but it was the condom on the pad at Cape Canaveral about to take off, with fire coming from down below, but nothing getting through. That was the point: The rocket couldn't get through, it was such a good condom. And a mate of mine wrote the slogan: 'Nothing Gets Through.' Short and sweet, eh? That's been kind of a theme in my life—not my *love* life, 'course, but everything else. And I got bounced out of there. . . . ''

Unlike so many rockers who go from disillusionment at school into the satisfaction of playing rock 'n' roll, though, Derek followed a reverse course, as it were. He had left a band called Skaface to enroll in LSD—although, as is so often the case, that wasn't the whole story.

"I was in Skaface twice, actually," Derek recalls after searching his memory with some effort. "I was in the original Skaface, thought I didn't really have a career in all that, so went to the LSD, did a year and a half, got back into Skaface, y'know, just when they were really beginning to happen. And it was a very thrilling couple of months."

As Derek remembers, it was thrilling in more ways than one—as opposed to the 2-Tone ska revival of a few years ago, white ska bands in the mid-Sixties were, to say the least, somewhat rare.

"It was dangerous, more than rare," he says. "Dangerous and, looking back on it, stupid. But it was exciting; we played a lot of Jamaican venues, and every once in a while we'd get a gig at the Marquee. And people wouldn't know what to think of us 'cause they'd say, 'What're these white boys playin'? What the fuck is *this* music?' 'Cause ska was not big then, among *anyone*—it was big in Jamaica, and we heard it on the radio and just sort of copied the arrangements."

Needless to say, by the time the ska revival came around, it was too late for the disbanded Skaface. "They didn't call *us, did* they?" Smalls reminisces ruefully.

Regrouping for another recollection, Derek faintly calls up memories of Milage, another pre-Tap unit that Smalls was with for one (and their only) album, *Milage I.*

"Milage was kind of a pre-Traffic Traffic. We had a flute player *and* a piccolo player, which was a *bit* much, I think, in the reed department. And then I played bass, we had a drummer and a guitarist—we tried to be heavier than we could, given the instrumentation. There was a lot of *lightness* in the band. Stevie McKechran was the lead singer, and then he went solo for a while. He's doin' a bit of advertising jingle work in London now, he's doin' all the milk jingles."

As the recollections come fewer and farther between, this trip down memory lane returns with an unexpected twist to Derek's days as a student at the LSD.

"It's ironic, isn't it? 'Cause I started out in advertising and got out. And Stevie started out in music and got *in.* 'Cause everything is so small over there; it's all one thing."

You could even say, in the words of Derek's own (never released) solo LP: *It's a Smalls World.* Somehow that figures.□

Taken from *Metälhead,* fall 1982

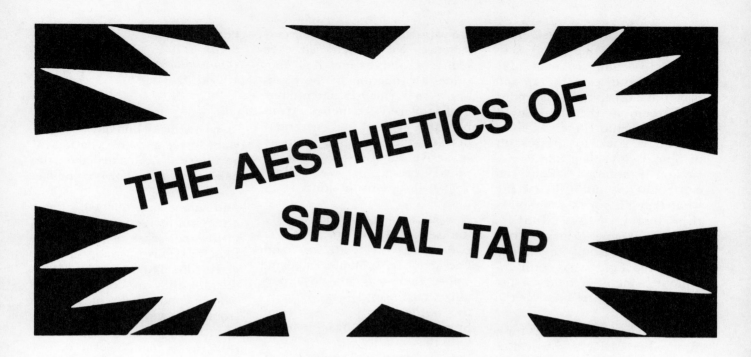

THE AESTHETICS OF SPINAL TAP

by R. Seltzer

The music trend business is a funny business. Once it was a matter of buying this Beatles album or that Stones single and figuring out where to go next, 'cause they and maybe Dylan and who else?—no one really—were leading the way and everybody else was a trillion miles behind. But then things really got weird and music trends in rock and roll began to have like these *half-lives*, like radioactive matter (and the key word there is radio 'cause that was before all this video rotgut). Dig, when you just had Chuck and Bo and Elvis and Jerry Lee then like there *weren't* any trends—you just had rock and roll, and even though we all said it'd last forever, it lasted, y'know, maybe ten, twelve years if we were lucky.

And then the Beatles lasted, c'mon, admit it, maybe six good years if you don't count *Let It Bleep* and *Abbey Bloat*—which I don't really—so who's counting?

Not me. Is it you? Is it? After that, people used Beatle albums for fans and dustpans. Reviewers sold their review copies to Sam Goody's unopened. So then you got glitter and glam and I give it three, four years with maybe six months added on for bad behavior. And we ain't even *talkin'* 'bout what was goin' on *this* side of the sea. So finally it got down to where these Brit-trends were subdividing like Levittown or something—when punk peaked after a couple years, and then there was just little neutron particles like 2 Tone ska revival and rockabilly revival and neo-psychedelia and poufta-rock and you name it 'cause I know you can.

The point being that all these little trendules sure looked nifty floatin' around but, like, their *half-lives* were getting smaller and smaller and shorter and shorter, so what's a poor rocker to do? Well, then longevity

becomes a thing of the past, dunnit? Yeah—that is, unless you're talkin' about a bunch o' boys been around as long as there's been rubber mats on turntables, seems to me, and that's the musical energy zap collective known as Spinal Tap.

Talk about half-lives, these cats got it down to a *science*, having broken down from, let's see here, Merseybeat ("Gimme Some Money") to Psychedelia/ Flower Power ("(Listen to the) Flower People," *We Are All Flower People*), Acid Rock (the live *Silent but Deadly*), Heavy Rock (*Brainhammer, Blood to Let, Nerve Damage, Intravenus de Milo*), Art Rock (the "concept" album *The Sun Never Sweats*), and finally various incarnations of Heavy Metal (*Jap Habit, Bent for the Rent, Shark Sandwich, Smell the Glove*).

Now what these albums all have in common besides David, Nigel and Derek ('cause the sidemen keep changin' like these self-destructo drummers, man, play on one, two discs with Tap and Bingo! it's off to that great play-back room in the sky—and if y'ask me would I like to maybe pick up the sticks for the next bit of Spinal vinyl then like Paulie says on "Revolution," "Baby, you can count me out"), like I say what they all got in common is this heavy, *heavy* duality, although I guess maybe you should call it *tri*ality, all things considered (and what with *tri*-athlons being *de rigueur* for the *nouvelle cuisine* set *this* week).

Let's see can we get serious for a minute here. OK? In a world of such things as randomness, onto-logical inconsistencies, and the constant unavoidable interruption of pure aesthetic perception by random happenings from within and without, not to mention the turnover in the average age of the (pop-) record-buying *pubic* [sic!] and fluctuations in the price of raw vinyl, eclec-ticism is the only valid position; and other stances may be meas-ured by virtue of their distance from the eclectic. (Hence the im-portance in rock and roll cos-mogony of the eclectic guitar, but more on that later.)

Teilhard de Chardin's philoso-phy of education as expounded in *The Phenomenon of Man* (must reading for every young proto-rocker) is readily visible in the eclecticism of rock. Just as Teilhard sees branches of life striving for continuation, some-times to succeed and sometimes to be lopped off by the cosmic random Gardener, with nature always using a multiplexity of interrelated strivings in its scor-ing drive toward the "Omega Point," rock and roll is clearly

viewable in terms of crude per-sistence. No branch can ever *really* become extinct if it con-tinues to function in the mem-ory, even dormantly, and old but undiscovered branches from both the "within" and "without" of things past can always appear in active functions in contem-porary rock, if we follow Teilhard's line of thinking. . . .

Now that wasn't so bad, was it? 'Cause what I'm gettin' at here is two words: "eclecticism" and "persistence." Memorize 'em, 'cause there's gonna be a pop quiz after the essay—no, actually this is the key to getting *inside* Spinal Tap. It also has lots to do with the "duality" (or "triality") that I mentioned before and that, with any luck at all, you've probably forgotten by now and more power to ya.

The almost forgotten minor 1965 semi-hit, f'rinstance, "Cups and Cakes" ("Oh what good things mother makes") features an ex-pectation of obscenity in its final verse:

I'm so full my tummy aches
How sad it must end
But I'm glad I've a friend
Sharing cups and cakes with me. *

The anticipation of sexual nour-ishment of such a like *specific* nature ("cups" as in C-cups, "cakes" as in James Brown's im-mortal line "For goodness sakes, take a look at those cakes!") is not too overtly common in rock and roll of this mid-Sixties era. But suddenly in the summer of 1973 we get more images of "cakes" popping up in "Big Bot-tom":

*All starred lyrics copyright © 1983 EmbCom Music Publishing (ASCAP). All rights reserved. Used by permission.

Big Bottom
Big Bottom
Talk about bum cakes
My gal's got 'em *

and again: "I saw her on Monday, 'twas my lucky bun day."* If you want to see a "bun" as a logical corollary of a "cake," then the baking/sex metaphor is complete.

And make no mistake, these dudes got food on the brain, like in the *root* sense of it in a song like "Sex Farm," man, they are gettin' down to the *means of pro-duction*, they are controllin' the whole Food Chain of Being—from "plowing through your beanfield" to "wolfing down some cornbread." Never before has the confluence of productiv-ity, consumption and conjugality flowed with more epistemolo-gically oiled conception, if you will, than in the line "Don't you see my silo risin' high."

In fact, the case can be made (and don't you just know I'm the guy to make it, babe!) that Spinal Tap have in their work mirrored the entire development of rock 'n' roll. They began with primitive emotional music ("Tonight I'm Gonna Rock You Tonight"), went on to hardcore affirmative kineticism ("Break like the Wind") and triviality (David's wail, "Go, Nigel, Go!" during "Gimme Some Money"), not to mention highly sophis-ticated arrogance (also "Gimme Some Money"), progressed to straightforward profundity ("Heavy Duty"), pessimism ("Hell Hole") and modern tragedy ("Rock and Roll Nightmare"), while relating themselves to the roots with revivals ("Rockin' Robin") and retrogressions to early noncogni-tiveness ("Get Me Away from the Ground" from *The Incredible*

Flight of Icarus P. Anybody, and later "Rock and Roll Creation").

All of which just goes to prove out the eternal virtually cosmic truth first verbalized in that immortal chestnut of the Riley-Farley Orchestra: "The Music Goes 'Round and Around"—which although written in 1936 (the year of "Gloomy Sunday," *Rhythm on the Range,* and "Rhythm Saved the World," how's that for research?) speaks backward to the evolution of the jazz era and forward to, well, Spinal Tap. 'Cause like the music *has* come 'round full circle to the point where not just four blokes from Liverpuddle but even two slobs from Squatney and a naif from Nilford-on-Null can grow up to be if not president of the United States at least hot shit rock 'n' rollers with stacks of Marshall amps to prove it by gum and not Only in America but in bloody England f'Chrissakes.

So let's hear if for the boys who put all of this year's model art-school rockers and pretentious psychepunkabilly revivalists and fashioncultmongers in their place with one stroke of their Gibsons and one howl of their atavistic, lustforlife lungs. But don't feel obliged to buy their albums. That would only spoil the fun—not to mention their position as unsung undersellers in the remainder bins of rock 'n' roll. Play 'em a dollar's worth of times down at the local pub. Or better yet, next time you're stuck in a crowded elevator, just whistle the chorus from "Heavy Duty" and watch the heads turn!

Berkeley, 1983 □

Reprinted from *Rock in a Nutshell: Critical Essays on Rock* (Samson Press, 1983).

In the course of preparing this book, I had the opportunity to converse by phone with Mr. Joe Franklin on the subject of Spinal Tap. Tap is one of literally hundreds of musical performers whom Joe has been responsible for exposing on a first-time basis to the American TV audience—even though they had been in existence for nearly twenty years prior to appearing on "The Joe Franklin Show." Still, Joe was quick to spot their potential, and his input doubtless improved their outlook, media-wise, in this country.

What follows here is a condensed version of our conversation, which foraged through many different fields but always returned to nibble contentedly on the foliaceous subjects of Spinal Tap and, of course, Joe Franklin himself.

AUTHOR: Hello, Mr. Franklin? I'm working on a book on a rock band called Spinal Tap, which made an appearance on your show last February.

JOE FRANKLIN: Ohhh, yeah. I think I might even still have that videotape of their appearance with me. I think I still have that.

AU: Well they quite enjoyed being on your show. Now I'm putting together this book as I say—

JF: Got a publisher already?

AU: It's for Arbor House.

JF: Ohh, they're a great company. I discovered them. The fellow who started the company isn't there anymore, but he came on my show with his first book—a man named Donald Fine. And he's not with the company anymore, but they gave him a good salary when they bought

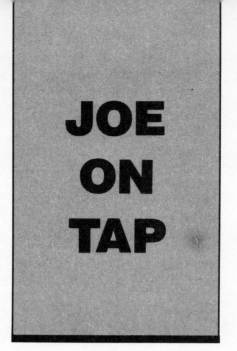

JOE ON TAP

him out. It's owned now by a very big house, I forget which one. . . .

AU: It's actually the Hearst Corporation.

JF: The Hearst Corporation, right. So you're with good people.

AU: I'll be including several interviews with the band in my book—

JF: Mine was their very first New York show, their very, very first.

AU: So, what I would like to do is—

JF: Sit with me, yeah.

AU: —print the transcript of their appearance on your show in the book. Now my publisher tells me I should get permission from you first.

JF: Absolutely. I'll tell you who to call. I just hope the show hasn't been erased—I pray to God it hasn't been erased. If not, I'll try and recount it from memory, you know what I'm saying?

AU: Oh, I believe I have a tape of it myself.

JF: Oh, that'd be sensational if you've got that. But you definitely have my permission. And the minute you're ready with the book, we'll kick it off on my show. I'll sell you fifteen thousand extra books. OK, m'boy?

AU: Well, of course, I'd be delighted. I've watched your show for many years and—

JF: Yeah, it's going great, going great. I want you to know that when the public-relations people called me to put them on, they told me they couldn't book them. They tried all over, they couldn't book 'em. They *pleaded*. So, y'know, they said, "Joe, we're gonna lose the account if you don't put them on." Do you know who the public-relations people were, by the way?

AU: I thought it was Nancy Seltzer Associates, for the movie.

JF: Somebody like that, but they couldn't get it. So I put 'em on, 'cause I'm a soft touch. And *then*, after *my* show, everybody wanted them. Didn't they go on "Live at Five" and all that kind of stuff? Evvv-ryone. I don't know what you're allowed to say about the power of my show, but if anybody goes on my show, they get picked up the next day by everybody. They all somehow very secretly monitor me, y'know? So you can play with that if you want to, it's up to you. Anything you want, OK, kid? And I'll send the release back by return mail.

AU: Thank you very much.

JF: Good luck with the book.

THE JOE FRANKLIN SHOW:

TAP ON JOE

(Excerpt from "The Joe Franklin Show," February 14, 1984)

JOE FRANKLIN: Evvv-rybody wants to hear Billy Bell, he's going to sing today and tomorrow. Now the Spinal Tap tell me they love the sound of WOR-TV Secaucus, New Jersey—What do you like about that word Secaucus, it's musical. . . ?

NIGEL TUFNEL: Yeah, it sort of lilts, dunnit?

DAVID ST. HUBBINS: It's got a cadence to it.

DEREK SMALLS: Indian word, isn't it?

FRANKLIN: Spinal Tap, you're going to be invited by a fantastic performer before you leave town to see *An Evening [at the Cotton Club]. . . .*

ST. HUBBINS: Ah, I *do* want to see that.

FRANKLIN: This man, I wanna tell you something: I loved him in *The Wiz* on Broadway, in *Don't Bother Me, I Can't Cope,* but what I saw the other night . . . Christophe, you're talking now to Spinal Tap and a lot of other people. Let's make some friends for a very exciting night.

CHRISTOPHE PIERRE: Yeah, come on out, we're at the Silver Lining—that's at 349 West Forty-sixth Street—Tuesday, Wednesday, Thursday, eight o'clock, Friday and Saturday, two shows, seven-thirty and ten-thirty, so come on out. . . .

FRANKLIN: Gimme one line of Cab Calloway, any one line of Cab Calloway, anything, Hi-de-ho, any one line. I know it's hard, but . . .

PIERRE: Uh [sings] "Hey, folks, here's a story 'bout Minnie the Moocher. . . ."

FRANKLIN: Ohhhhh, you are, you are . . . oohhh . . .

PIERRE: And it's exciting because of the white hat and the whole idea. . . .

FRANKLIN: You are a dazzler, I mean that. And what might Bert Williams say, if the late and great Bert Williams were . . .

PIERRE: [Sings] "Come after breakfast, Bring your own lunch, But leave before suppertime."

FRANKLIN: That is so exciting. *An Evening at the Cotton Club.*

(Collection of the author.)

ST. HUBBINS: Those are all both real people . . . I've heard of Cab Calloway, but the other, uh . . .

PIERRE: Bert Williams? Bert was an exciting character player. He would get out and he would do all things like "Old Jasper Green, Deacon of the Church," and he was always with hands, everything that he did was hands, and gloves. He was an exciting character—movement, always movement. . . .

FRANKLIN: An exciting man named Christophe Pierre. There's a major motion-picture documentary, my friends, being released in New York and Los Angeles on March 2 entitled *This Is Spinal Tap.* And Spinal Tap's concerts, I guess, and gold albums are kind of legendary in England, and in many parts of the world internationally. But my question is, Will there eventually be an American Spinal Tap cross-country tour, gentlemen? *Maybe.*

ST. HUBBINS: Yes.

TUFNEL: Well, uh, yeah. . . .

ST. HUBBINS: We're discussing it. Just a few wrinkles to iron out and I think we're ready.

SMALLS: People are on the phone right now, working on it.

ST. HUBBINS: Could've played here before, but, oh, number of years ago when we had a hit record, almost twenty years ago.

FRANKLIN: You're a baby. Courtesy of David St. Hubbins, and Nigel . . .

TUFNEL: Tufnel.

FRANKLIN: . . . Tufnel, and Derek Smalls, here is a sample of a forthcoming movie called *This Is Spinal Tap,* and I'm very excited to say: This is a first. Lean back, gentlemen, and watch yourselves in brilliant 3-D.

[A clip of Spinal Tap singing "(Listen to the) Flower People," c. 1967, is shown.]

FRANKLIN: Mr. Christophe

Pierre was just asking me, Bruce Logan, if the music we just heard —and saw, saw and heard—by Spinal Tap was kind of, uh, "flower power." Is that the word, "flower power"?

ST. HUBBINS: Right, that's pretty much what it represents as far as a form of music, yes. What we do now is a bit more heavy rock 'n' roll, good-time rock 'n' roll.

SMALLS: Bashin'.

FRANKLIN: How important is video in building up young stars today?

TUFNEL: Oh, extremely, extremely important.

ST. HUBBINS: More and more.

FRANKLIN: More notoriety, more audience, more everything, right?

TUFNEL: Yeah.

ST. HUBBINS: Well, not necessarily notoriety, but at least an attraction; it's important, I think.

TUFNEL: Yeah.

FRANKLIN: What do you think, Chri—yeah? [Points to Smalls]

SMALLS: Who, me?

FRANKLIN: Yes.

SMALLS: Yeah, it's very important.

FRANKLIN: But, Christophe, uh?

PIERRE: Yah, because I'm in hopes now of getting "Cotton Club" like, on a video, because it's so exciting—

ST. HUBBINS: That'd be great.

PIERRE: —it could become a piece of history. Because everybody can't make the clubs and see, but just to have that to work *from*. It's so exciting, then you can see and really get some power going. . . .

FRANKLIN: I think Bruce Logan of *TV Shopper*, with a young fellow named *me* on the cover, wanted to mention a movie. You want them to catch a certain movie called *Broadway Danny Rose*?

BRUCE LOGAN: Yes, absolutely, yes.

ST. HUBBINS: Ah, yes, I plan to. I adore his films.

TUFNEL: That's, uh, Woody Allen, right?

ST. HUBBINS: I adore his films.

LOGAN: And as a matter of fact there was a marvelous write-up about it in the current issue of *New York* magazine—

ST. HUBBINS: Right. Right, saw it in the hotel.

LOGAN: —in which Joe Franklin was prominently mentioned as one of the major—his show was mentioned as one of the major spawning grounds of talent that is someday going to become something in this country.

FRANKLIN: Ladies and gentlemen, I've got a friend, one of my first friends ever in TV, and the Spinal Tap members and Christophe Pierre and Bruce Logan tell me that they are fans of country music. And this man is in the Hall of Fame—he is a young immortal. He's been touring through the years with *every*-body, and headlining with everybody; he's a very good friend of Merle Haggard. . . . And here is Billy Bell to sing a Merle Haggard song, from the album called *Roses in the Winter*, a good friend, Billy Bell. OK, Billy.

[Billy Bell is shown singing "Roses in the Winter."]

FRANKLIN: Billy Bell, Billl-ly Bellllll will sing again tomorrow. I've been told this is the seventeenth album by the Spinal Tap? [Shows album jacket.]

ST. HUBBINS: That's right.

FRANKLIN: First of all I want to thank Mr. Christophe Pierre for dropping in and inviting our friends to bring back highlight recollections of *An Evening at the Cotton Club* in midtown Manhattan, the Silver Lining. I want to thank Mr. Bruce Logan for the honor—I wanna tell you that the man who *wrote* the article, Richard Schwartz, should drop down here one day, because he's bright.

LOGAN: He's interviewed a lot of people; not as many as you, Joe, but, uh, he would be very interesting.

FRANKLIN: What is your final thought for the gentlemen known as Spinal Tap?

LOGAN: Oh, I just was curious. Did you three know each other as children, like the Beatles when they were growing up?

TUFNEL: [pointing to St. Hubbins]: *We* did. We grew up together in London.

LOGAN: I just gathered that, I just felt it, uh. That's wonderful.

FRANKLIN: Did you begin "gigging," as they say, in local pubs?

ST. HUBBINS: Yeah, mostly outside of tube stations. Subway stops.

TUFNEL: Some small clubs as well, yeah.

(Collection of the author.)

ST. HUBBINS: "Skiffle groups," we called them then. It was like jug bands over here.

FRANKLIN: And stuff like that, heh heh. Mr. Pierre, what do you want to ask of a red-hot group?

PIERRE: Uh, a question I was just thinking about as I heard your tape? I was wondering, just in comparison to the sound that I heard and the sound that you're doing now, how would you say that you've changed over completely? You're still going to go back to the old sound of yester—

ST. HUBBINS: That's a very good question.

SMALLS: You know, we're a lot heavier, there's more *power* in the music today.

TUFNEL: Yeah, everything's louder today, really, mostly.

ST. HUBBINS: And it's a matter of audience demand, really. I mean—

PIERRE: Yeah, because I was wondering, because there *is* a market for the sound that you had before.

ST. HUBBINS: Oh, is that so? We'll bring it back.

SMALLS: We'll re-release it.

ST. HUBBINS: It never goes stale, you know.

PIERRE: It works very well for you.

ST. HUBBINS: Great. Thank you very much.

SMALLS [to Franklin]: Well, we know you like nostalgia, so that's why we brought *that* clip. [Theme music comes up.]

FRANKLIN: Did you say nostalgia or neuralgia? Nostalgia. Ladies and gentlemen, this has been for me an hour of hours. We'll, uh, always be, uh, in touch and, uh, admiring these fantastic entertainers. Have a good day, and a good night, and do stay well. And don't get any spinal taps. They hurt.

ST. HUBBINS: Oh, yes.

FRANKLIN: No spinal taps.

ST. HUBBINS: Only *our* kind.

FRANKLIN: Huh-huh.

[Theme music up full]

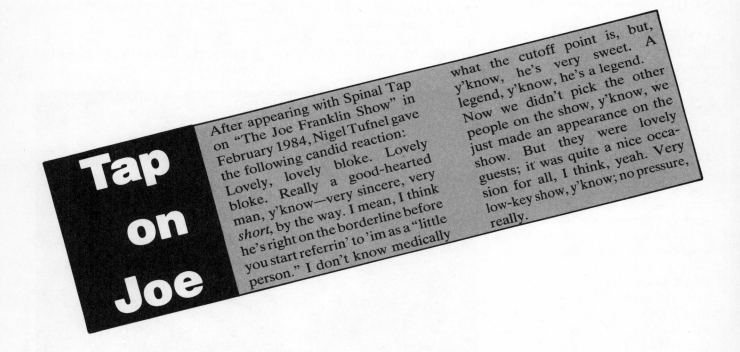

Tap on Joe

After appearing with Spinal Tap on "The Joe Franklin Show" in February 1984, Nigel Tufnel gave the following candid reaction: Lovely, lovely bloke. Lovely bloke. Really a good-hearted man, y'know—very sincere, very *short*, by the way. I mean, I think he's right on the borderline before you start referrin' to 'im as a "little person." I don't know medically what the cutoff point is, but, y'know, he's very sweet. A legend, y'know, he's a legend. Now we didn't pick the other people on the show, y'know, we just made an appearance on the show. But they were lovely guests; it was quite a nice occasion for all, I think, yeah. Very low-key show, y'know; no pressure, really.

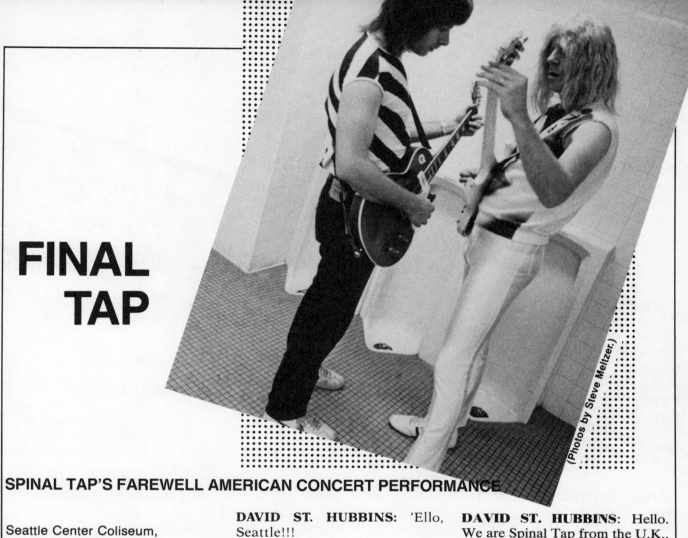

(Photos by Steve Meltzer.)

FINAL TAP

SPINAL TAP'S FAREWELL AMERICAN CONCERT PERFORMANCE

Seattle Center Coliseum,
Seattle, Washington

DAVID ST. HUBBINS: 'Ello, Seattle!!!

["Tonight I'm Gonna Rock You Tonight" is performed, following which the band begins tuning up at length.]

DAVID ST. HUBBINS: Hello. We are Spinal Tap from the U.K., you must be the USA!... A brief hiatus for the members tuning ... We'd like to welcome you all. We understand we are breaking in this hall, so let's really break it in,

will we?!! You know we've come a long way.

DEREK SMALLS: Yeah!!

DAVID ST. HUBBINS: We've come a long way. We've been here once before—in the year of nineteen and sixty-seven as a matter of fact. More about that later on.

eleven!...Eleven! Eleven! Eleven! Eleven! Thank you!

[The crowd takes up the chant of "E-LEV-en! E-LEV-en! E-LEV-en! E-LEV-en! E-LEV-en!"]

Let's hear it for him; he doesn't have to do this!

Backstage, Seattle Center Coliseum.

NIGEL TUFNEL: Good to be back!...We'll tune a bit more for you later....Uh, we'd like to do—the next tune we're gonna do is something I wrote with my, uh, dear partner, David St. Hubbins....

ST. HUBBINS: Play the Nigel Tufnel intro.

["Hell Hole" is performed.]

TUFNEL: Thank you very much!

SMALLS: "Hell Hole," thank you.

ST. HUBBINS: Great to see music without pictures again, innit?

SMALLS: Hello, Bremerton!

TUFNEL: We're gonna try to build this 'ere one up to

ST. HUBBINS: Well, then... Y'know, it really is gratifyin'. The last time we were comin' through here, we had trouble playin' over at Duke's. But now that we're 'ere and 'avin' a bit of notoriety on account of the film, we can really be a bit self-indulgent, and tell you how much we *love* you. Thank you very much for comin' out here today....We'd like now for you to thrust your minds back into those five minutes right before the creation of the universe— you recall, it was in all the papers.

["Rock and Roll Creation" is performed.]

ST. HUBBINS: "Rock and Roll Creation." Thank you very much. Something to think about, isn't it...? And now, to prove the drum solo is not dead yet— Mr. Richard...Shrimpton!!!

[Shrimpton performs a short drum solo.]

TUFNEL: Yes he does.

ST. HUBBINS: On the bass, Mr. Derek Smalls....On the bass, Mr. Nigel Tufnel....On the bass keyboards, Mr. Viv Savage.... My name is David St. Hubbins, lead bass....

["Big Bottom" is performed, at the end of which Smalls and St. Hubbins rhythmically whack Tufnel in the bum with their instruments.]

ST. HUBBINS: And let that be a lesson to ya, Nige!...There are those who say the guitar solo is a thing of the past. There are those who say it's obsolete, it's dead, it's boring, been done. Proving them wrong literally single-handedly...Mr....Nigel... Tufnel!

[Tufnel plays a brief, derivative

guitar solo, which leads into a performance of "Heavy Duty."]

ST. HUBBINS: Thank you very much. "Heavy Duty, Heavy duty rock 'n' roll, Heavy duty, Brings out the duty in my soul"—yes, words worth living by. How're you all feeling tonight, eh? [Crowd cheers.] No, no, one at a time, one at a time, starting with you . . . [points]. Nah, that'll take all day, won't it? You are a good-looking group, I must say, though —let's see your profile. Yeah, everybody turn sideways. . . .

TUFNEL: Turn this way.

ST. HUBBINS: Everybody turn this way. . . .

TUFNEL: Turn this way.

ST. HUBBINS: Not that way yet. *This* way first.

TUFNEL: And then *this* way.

ST. HUBBINS: That's OK.

SMALLS: Good noses, good noses.

ST. HUBBINS: Yeah, you look like ya should have little numbers under your chests when you do that, somehow.

TUFNEL: Ah, the next tune we'd like to do—

ST. HUBBINS: Hey, wait a second!

TUFNEL: Oh, sorry!

ST. HUBBINS: Where's Pam and Neil? Oh, OK, I'm glad you made it.

TUFNEL: Uh, this next tune we're doing is a suite that I wrote—*Thank* you!—and, uh, y'know, bein' from Squatney and all, it's a pleasure to be in this great country, and, uh, we hope you enjoy it. And if you don't, it really doesn't matter that much, frankly.

["America" is performed.]

ST. HUBBINS: Our way of saying, Thank you, America! . . . Another quick tuning session, it'll only take a moment. This is going to take you back a few years—it does *us*. This is to a time when most of you had not yet been born. . . . P'raps you were made while your parents were listening to this tune. But it's not mere nostalgia, because the best of the old can become the best of the new through rearranging. . . .

[A version of "(Listen to the) Flower People" is performed, to a reggae beat.]

Any last-minute requests?

[Crowd shouts a number of largely inaudible song titles.]

All right. OK. All right, we'll do 'em all, we'll do 'em all.

TUFNEL: Wait, wait, wait. Wai-wai-wai-wai-wait! "Stranger in the Night" in D?

SMALLS: D-*minor.*

completely passed away yet. Y'know? Because back in—no . . . when I was *your* age, when I

was *your* age, it was in doubt, because the only thing they had over here in the States was Bobby Vinton and Bobby Vee and Bobby Goldsboro, and more bloody Bobbys than you could shake a stick at. . . . And then those four blokes from Liverpool—I've forgotten their names—they sort of

["Gimme Some Money" is performed. During the song, many coins are flung at the band, some whistling just past their heads. At this point, St. Hubbins calls for the house lights to come up, and exhorts the audience to sing along—perhaps in the expectation that they can't sing and visibly throw coins at the same time.]

ST. HUBBINS: Louder!

[Crowd chants, "Gimme some mo-ney!"]

You don't sound like capitalists to *me*! That's more like it! [Song ends.] Thank you. In Detroit they threw *paper* money—and no one's got a job in Detroit. . . . How ya doin' there? This is a great-looking crowd, I must say. You know, you're all quite young. . . .

SMALLS: Almost young enough!

ST. HUBBINS: You know, many of you weren't even on the planet when those last songs were presented. But I'm glad to say that rock 'n' roll has not

inspired all of us, all of us we were sitting at home, squeezin' our spots in the mirror, y'know, and goin', "Wonder when this adolescent shit is gonna be *done* with?" y'know, and sayin'—

TUFNEL: 'Ey, David—

ST. HUBBINS: —well, get yourself an electric guitar.

TUFNEL: 'Ey, David, what you talkin' about?

ST. HUBBINS: I dunno, it's prob'ly the drugs.

TUFNEL: [Laughs] He's ramblin' on and on. Uh, what he's tryin' to say is this is one of our most classic numbers. It's about, uh, history really. It goes way back in time. I think you know what we're about.

["Stonehenge" is performed.]

SMALLS: Thank you, lovers of history!

ST. HUBBINS: Thank you very much. . . . If you ever go to Eng-

land, you should be sure and visit the monuments at Stonehenge. It's marvelous—if you haven't been overhyped, it's wonderful. . . . And when you're in Los Angeles, visit Universal Studios. . . . Is it loud enough?

[Crowd yells "No!"]

Whaaat? We'd better turn it UPP! You've been very kind. We need some more requests, though. Any other Spinal Tap favorites you'd like to hear? . . . Good one! Y'know, there's been

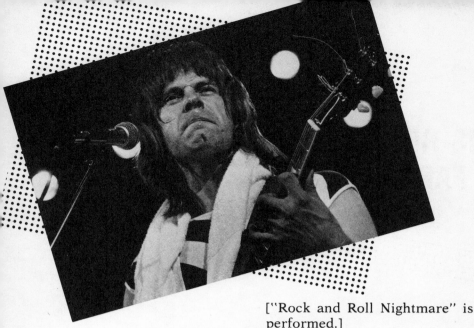

ST. HUBBINS: Mr. Nigel Tufnel and myself wrote this song nearly twenty-two years ago. We're so bloody sick of it, we thought you might like it, too.

["All the Way Home" is performed.]

ST. HUBBINS: Thank you very

a lot of controversy about the lyrics of this song—I don't personally see it. We'd like you to be the judge, so keep your ears open . . . and mind your back flap.

["Sex Farm" is performed.]

ST. HUBBINS: Thank you. Thank you. We should like to finish off our portion now of the Bumbershoot festivities with a journey into the inner heart and the very twisted soul of rock 'n' roll. And we'd like to propel you once again—dream-style—into the rock 'n' roll nightmare.

["Rock and Roll Nightmare" is performed.]

ST. HUBBINS: Thank you very much!!! Thank you all, bless your ass, and g'night!!

TUFNEL: Thank you very much for comin'!

[Spinal Tap exit to modest applause, and quickly reemerge from the wings.]

ST. HUBBINS: Thank you! There now, that didn't take long, *did* it? "Rockin' Robin!" Lead vocals Mr. Nigel Tufnel!

["Rockin' Robin" is performed.]

TUFNEL: Yeah, thank you! You've probably seen *this* gesture before—everyone goes CRAZY! Well, about twenty people, anyway.

much. We'd like to leave you now with a new American classic, one of those songs that's as timeless as, well rock 'n' roll. In-nit timeless?

[Bruce Springsteen's "Pink Cadillac" is performed.]

DAVID, NIGEL, DEREK: Thank you, thank you very much and goodnight, America!

DAVID ST. HUBBINS REMINISCES ON SPINAL TAP'S FAREWELL CONCERT IN SEATTLE

Q: How was the concert in Seattle?

DAVID: It was just great. A whole trainload of kids showed up. A lot of fun—played the old hits, you know, and we played one Bruce Springsteen song, too. Played "Pink Cadillac," just to see what they'd do. They were confused, but they liked it, they like being confused.

Q: You didn't even have a black sax player, did you?

DAVID: No, right. Well, actually there was one in the audience, but we had nothing to do with him—he just showed up, you know. You play a certain kind of music, black horn players come out of the woodwork—it's amazing.

Q: Is this a first for Tap, playing a cover version?

DAVID: Oh, no, we used to do covers all the time. Of course, like all R&B-oriented groups, we used to do, y'know, "Shakin' All Over" and "Route 66" and all those great old classics. And we've always done "Rockin' Robin."

Q: But this is a first in terms of covering a contemporary tune, no?

DAVID: Yes, I believe it is, as a matter of fact. No, actually, not true. . . . In '68 we did a cover of "Lady Madonna." It wasn't really successful, but we did give it a try. Got a fair response from the punters, but . . . I don't think we really had the light touch for it.

NIGEL ON THE SEATTLE CONCERT

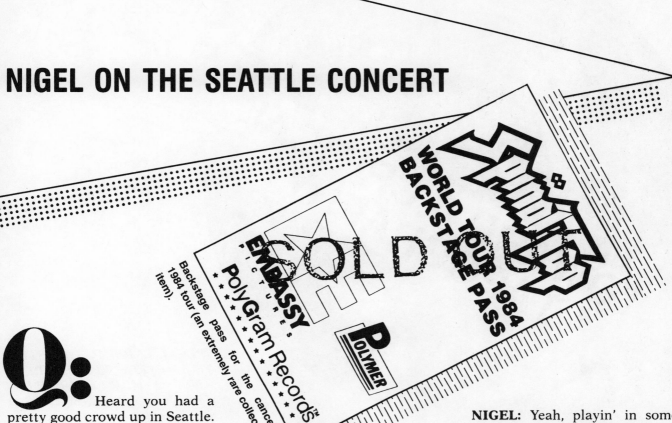

Backstage pass for the canceled 1984 tour (an extremely rare collector's item).

Q: Heard you had a pretty good crowd up in Seattle.

NIGEL: Yeah, huge—humongous crowd. They were pretty well behaved. They weren't throwing anything until "Gimme Some Money," and then they really let loose with a lot of change.

Q: That sounds like it could be dangerous, no?

NIGEL: Yeah, well, I normally sing on the tune, and I was forced to have a hasty retreat upstage towards the drummer, and I just turned my back. And really, it's not as painful taking it off the back of the head as in the lip. I got one in the lip in Detroit that was quite painful.

Q: Heard there were some problems in Boston as well on this tour.

NIGEL: Yeah, playin' in some stupid club where the roof was leakin', and it was rainin' on stage and, y'know, I don't normally play in a Mac—so we had to sort of strong-arm the little twit into making it *not* rain, really. We just said we're not playin' in the rain, it's quite simple. Y'know, it'd be our last gig if we did that, being electrocution thing and all that.

TOWARD A CRITICAL TAPOGRAPHY

Throughout their chameleonic history, Spinal Tap have been consistent in one sense—aside, that is, from always being ever so slightly behind the beat, both rhythmically and stylistically. What I mean is, they've always been more of an album band than a singles band. Certainly this jibes with the AOR format that has historically given full creative leeway to their extraordinary flights of sheer solo *endurance*. But before rating the albums, a few words need to be said about the trusty old 45s that first got the band boogeying down.

Beginning with the classic Merseybeat sound of "Gimme Some Money" b/w "Cups and Cakes" (Abbey, 1965), recorded as the Thamesmen with Ronnie Pudding on bass, through their misty-eyed tributes to flower-power/psychedelia in "(Listen to the) Flower People" and the rarely heard "Rainy Day Sun" (Megaphone, 1967), their early days are marked by an almost painful simplicity of style, verging, quite frankly, on emptiness. And this was years before Lennon and McCartney penned their classic "Nowhere Man." However void of extraneous trappings these early sides may be, they still contain the germ of Tap's more elaborate output. Now let's rock on.

SPINAL TAP SINGS "(LISTEN TO THE) FLOWER PEOPLE" AND OTHER FAVORITES (Originally released in England as *Spinal Tap*. Megaphone, 1967). Clear, crisp, scintillating, the first fresh breath of a new dawn sweeping over the sludgy, self-satisfied rooftops of rock 'n' roll. Or was it a new, gritty realism putting the lie to the prettified homogeneity of early-Sixties "Bobbie" rock? Who cares? We know vintage gold when we smell it. What's really amazing is how well this stuff has aged. Our advice: Buy a few cases and lay them down in the cellar for your grandkids. Standouts include the mellow title track and the wryly portentous "Have a Nice Death," featuring a killer drum solo from "Stumpy" Pepys. **A**+

WE ARE ALL FLOWER PEOPLE (Megaphone, 1968). When a flower begins to fade, it gives off a faintly sickly smell, and much the same could be said for Tap's attempt to cash in on their surprisingly successful debut LP. If that one was premier cru Bordeaux, this is pure red ink. A few of the songs were molded around a questionable proto-concept: the story of a lad who, like ill-fated Icarus, decided that he would put on wings and fly—except that he would be a kind of human airliner and sell seats on himself to pay for the project. Needless to say, the boys were "heavy into acid" at the time. When sales proved as disappointing as the concept, the LP was retitled *The Incredible Flight of Icarus P. Anybody* and reissued minus the original title track. The new title, however, proved eerily prophetic as far as chart position was concerned. **C-**

SILENT BUT DEADLY (Megaphone, 1969). Tap are, needless to say, the pre-eminent live band, as this LP, recorded at the Electric Zoo, Whimpton, conclusively hints. I say "hints" because, due to the classic short-sightedness of the button-down nerds at Megaphone, the meta-legendary two-hour Tufnel–St. Hubbins twin guitar solo on "Short and Sweet" was chopped to a niggardly 18:37. Fortunately, some bootlegs exist (see below), and despite poor sound quality, are worth ferreting out. Humorous highlight: the snap-crackle-pop sound effects during Nigel's spoken intro to "Breakfast of Evil." **B+**

BRAINHAMMER (Megaphone, 1970). Here the band has clearly hit their lumbering stride full tilt, moving with the lean, mean aplomb of a brontosaurus in fighting trim. "Big Bottom," one of their earliest evergreens, brilliantly foreshadows Queen's later lesser ode to the bum cheek, "Fat-Bottomed Girls." Allegations of sexism miss the point—as Derek once explained, the song doesn't demean women but merely a part of their anatomy. Also delectable for the sheer brute force of their execution are "Lie Back and Take It" and the sultry "Swallow My Love." **A**

NERVE DAMAGE (Megaphone, 1971), *BLOOD TO LET* (Megaphone, 1972), *INTRAVENUS DE MILO* (Megaphone, 1974). Alas, a certain, how shall I say, *sameness* has set in during this period of the band's meteoric rise to the middle of the pack. Apart from a hard-rockin' "Tonight I'm Gonna Rock You Tonight" and the devilishly witty deconstruction of Social Darwinism, "Saliva of the Fittest" on *Intravenus*, not much of substance has survived from this three-year musical backwater. But hey, they're entitled. **B-**

THE SUN NEVER SWEATS (Megaphone, 1975). Ponderous is the word for this late-blooming concept album that only a Taphead could love, padded as it is with creaky period pieces ("Daze of Knights of Old") and too-precious Donovan knock-offs ("The Princess and the Unicorn," "The Obelisk"). Riding the rising tide of British chauvinism implied in the title (see ADDENDUM), Tap end up sounding, in the words of the overwrought title song, like "the hardest concrete" that "never quite sets." But when Tap stumble, at least they stumble big. Their nostalgic orgy of Britannophilia, which also brought us the deathless mytho-historico-romance "Stonehenge," is further proof that this fine band's reach sometimes exceeded its gasp. "Even the biggest elephant never forgets," David sings; in sooth, prithee forget this one, lads. **C**

JAP HABIT (Megaphone, 1975). Triple-live barnburner that shouts a loud *banzai!* in the face of anyone who had lost faith in Tap's ability to soldier through the dreariest of times. Other bands may have already been cranking out double and triple live LPs in Far Eastern venues, but Tap's is somehow, well, longer and louder than most. Former session drummer Peter "James" Bond provides a welcome (if short-lived) steadiness to the ever-turbulent percussion chair, and Ross MacLochness churns out some monster (no pun intended) keyboard riffs on the breakneck "Devil Take the Hindmost" and the dreamy instrumental "Nocturnal Mission." But "Nice 'n' Stinky" proved to be the sleeping time-bomb that would explode into unexpected mega-hitdom two years later in the US. **B+**

BENT FOR THE RENT (Megaphone, 1976). With the exception of the memorably anthemic "Heavy Duty" ("No page in history, baby—that I don't need/I just want to make some eardrums bleed"), this tardy entry in the glitter-rock sweepstakes is best forgotten. Ask yourself if you really want to hear Tap perform titles like the ill-conceived glam-soul pastiche "When a Man Looks Like a Woman," or the New York Dolls/Mitch Ryder homage, "High Heels, Hot Wheels." Nor did the LP go very far toward paying David, Nigel, and Derek's respective rents, for that matter. **C-**

ROCK AND ROLL CREATION (Megaphone, 1977). Score one for the bean-counters. Tap may even have got the idea for the infamous *Smell the Glove* cover when their former label "rubbed their noses in it" by releasing this shoddy collection of rejected tracks after the band's much publicized lawsuit against Megaphone. Was it gratuitous irony on Megaphone's part to include an especially off-key version of the band's rarely performed punk excursion, "Young, Smug and Famous"? We won't dignify the bastards by giving this one a rating.

NIGEL TUFNEL'S CLAM CARAVAN (Plutarch, 1979). Ah, yes, the solo albums, product of Tap's banishment from Megaphone and their near-legendary sojourn in Nigel's Scottish castle. To be perfectly honest, the infelicitously mistitled *Clam Caravan* (the label should've read "Calm") is right up there with such fish-out-of-water efforts as Bill Wyman's *A Stone Alone* and Ross MacLochness's *Doesn't Anybody Here Speak English*? Just as MacLochness's solo LP sprang from his experience of missionary work in Namibia, Nigel's exotic sound-trip to the North African desert seems to emerge from some dark, arid patch of his troubled psyche. If this is any indication of the sheer torpor of Tap's collective dark night of the soul, it's probably just as well that Derek's solo opus, *It's a Smalls World*, never saw the fluorescent light of record stores. **C-**

SHARK SANDWICH (Polymer, 1980). Having languished a significant three years in the tomb-like limbo of contractual lawsuits and solo maunderings, Tap are luminously resurrected here with a new label, a new direction, and (natch) a new drummer. A joyously nihilistic "No Place Like Nowhere" and their late-disco hit "Throb Detector" lead the way. But the sheer suggestive brilliance of "Sex Farm" presages their eventual ascension into Heavy Metal Heaven. Who needs the self-serving "Wild Man" posturings of today's trendy Iron John set when we can hear Tap singing about *real* men swinging real pitchforks? You'd have to go clear back to Breughel for an equally heady brew of hard-working everyman earthiness and primal barnyard lust. We can almost see the steam rising off the cow chips on this one. **A+**

SMELL THE GLOVE (Polymer, 1982). They may have come out of the depths, but their reminiscences of that tedious time still burn on in the thundering "Hell Hole." Yet the band seem curiously ambivalent: are they glad to be out of a place where "the rats are peeling," or are they even more nauseated by the high life they've regained, however briefly ("The sauna's drafty, the pool's too hot/The kitchen stinks of boiling snails")? *You* figure it out. As for the notoriously suppressed cover and lurid title track, gimme a break! Tap as misogynists? Smell *this*, buddy! **B+**

THIS IS SPINAL TAP— THE SOUNDTRACK (Polymer, 1984). More of a greatest hits package—albeit with many of their later tunes given new live treatments—than a bold step forward. Still, the LP does have one unassailable advantage over most of the others reviewed here: IT'S STILL IN PRINT! **A-**

BREAK LIKE THE WIND (Dead Faith/MCA, 1992). Tap's first new LP in a decade presents both the ultimate enigma and the ultimate challenge to their credibility. Daringly interlarding hot new tracks in the band's reborn molten metal style ("Bitch School," "Cash on Delivery") with classic period pieces ("The Sun Never Sweats," "Clam Caravan," "All the Way Home"), *BLTW* offers a uniquely valuable panorama of the band's development. But it also begs the question, Have Tap Sold Out? Squeaky clean production values, all-star guest soloists like Jeff Beck, Steve Lukather, Dweezil Zappa, and Cher(!), flawless engineering, and socially relevant issues ranging from ecology ("Stinking Up the Great Outdoors") to euthanasia ("Track 13")—are these the qualities we've come to expect from England's Loudest Band? The real payoff just may be "Rainy Day Sun," a deliriously psychedelic foreshadowing of Kinks/Small Faces/Beatles modalities that was the original B-side of "Flower People." The story is that the 1967 tune was yanked by the band after "I Am the Walrus" and "Itchycoo Park" came out, so as "not to cause confusion in the marketplace," and was never included on its debut LP. How fitting that Tap's one legitimate chance to be ahead of its time ended up as an obscure collector's item until 25 years *after* its time! Overall, I'm strongly ambivalent about this one, but I'll give it the benefit of the doubt: as with the previous LP, you can actually buy it in stores. **A**

"... and the prayers of devils fill the midnight sky." (Photo by Sylvia Otte.)

Bootlegger's Paradise

Strictly speaking, I don't condone the practice of bootlegging records, which deprives the artists (not to mention various industry bloodsuckers) of their rightful royalties, however meager. Let's face it, bootleggers are repugnant parasites who stink up the world of pop music even worse than some agents do. But in the case of Spinal Tap, sheer pragmatism dictates that, if you ever want to hear more than the occasional hit single collected on their two extant LPs, you'd better stick a clothes pin on your nose and go rooting through the nearest bootleg bin. Ads for used Tap LPs do sometimes appear in collectors' journals like *Goldmine*, but due to often scanty original sales, don't expect to find much there. To help you in your search, I humbly offer my Fab Five.

1. *Audible Death* (Gaswind, 1969). Sounds like someone had a small cassette recorder in about the 50th row of the Electric Zoo the same day *Silent but Deadly* was recorded. Audio quality is zilch, and the constant sound of someone choking on what must have been incredibly bad dope is distracting, but it's worth a shot, if only for the justly famous two-hour "Short and Sweet."

2. *Live at Budokkan* (Japtap, 1975). In case you didn't get enough to feed your *Jap Habit,* this Budokkan's for you. Stellar acoustics, although some overheated fan keeps screaming *Bonzai!* in the middle of Nigel's guitar solos. A mixed blessing, but more blessed than mixed.

3. *Got Thamesmen on Tap* (Merseybleat, ND). If our ears don't lie, this is historic stuff, with Ronnie Pudding and a pre-gardening accident "Stumpy" Pepys in top form. Early hits and a cool smattering of cover versions, purportedly taped in an underground club in Rotterdam. On the other hand, it may just be an incredible simulation, which pretty much amounts to the same thing.

4. *It's a Dub World* (Skaface, 1979?). The bass tracks *only* to Derek's never-released solo LP, somehow pirated from the studio where he was working at the time. Lets the imagination run wild.

5. *Openfaced Mako* (Hammerhead, 1980). A collection of outtakes from the *Shark Sandwich* sessions, replete with some *very* revealing in-studio banter (near-fistfights would be more like it!). A real must, especially for the never-released, XXX-rated version of "Sex Farm." Naughty, naughty.

Q: While we have a moment here, I'd like to straighten out a few things I've always wanted to know about Spinal Tap's recordings over the years. First off, I'd like to ask you, Derek, what exactly *The Incredible Flight of Icarus P. Anybody* (originally titled *We Are All Flower People*) was all about.

DEREK: It was a very, very early concept album about a man who decided, like Icarus, that he would put on wings and fly—but that he would be a jet airliner and that he would sell seats on himself to pay for the project. You know, it was very acid-influenced: One of the songs was "To Fly," another one was "I Am Flight," it was all on the subject *of* flight. It was probably the heaviest use of Mellotron up until that time on a rock 'n' roll album, which idea was stolen from us by you know who—by you know Moody who. But we did it *first*, and I think we got some sort of award from the Mellotron people for it, because it was really thick with Mellotron, it was all the way through. It just covered everything, like a Mellotron soup—which gave the album a distinctive kind of murk.

A lot of it was that we were doing some bass work on the Mellotron, just some bass chords—because that was describing the *ground* that Icarus was trying to escape from: "Get Me Away from the Ground," I believe, was Cut Two, Side One. So there was this brooding sense of the ground that was in these heavy, thick fifths being played down in the bass range of the Mellotron. It was very, very dark. Basically

Backstage. (Photos by Steve Meltzer.)

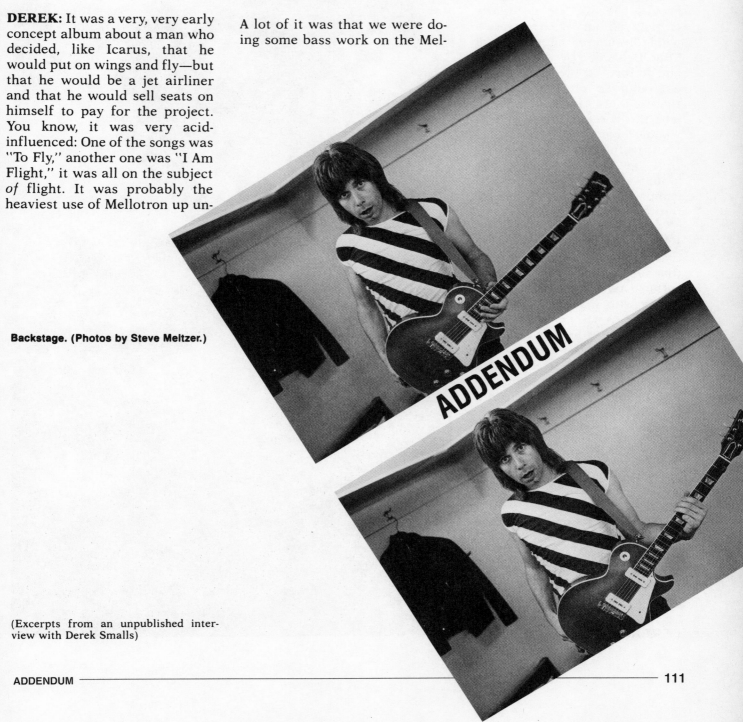

ADDENDUM

(Excerpts from an unpublished interview with Derek Smalls)

it just thickened things up a bit, it was a thickener—like musical cornstarch, in a way.

Q: While we're on the subject of concept albums, I'm not sure I ever fully understood the concept behind your most famous concept LP, *The Sun Never Sweats*.

DEREK: People have always said that to us over here, because it was a peculiarly British album. There was a whole round of campaigns of "Buy British," "Up the British," and so forth at the time. And at one point we felt, Right, we *are* British, there's no escaping that; let's throw our lot in with this, y'know? For a while there was even the thought that maybe we could get it to be the official album of the "Up the British" campaign. But then the board felt that it was too hardcore.

But it was basically just saying that the empire was a good idea, that subjugating foreign peoples —there was nothing really wrong with that. That the dark and the small peoples *were* meant to serve us. It was taking the stance of the band, which was a stance of strength and power and domination, and saying, Yeah, well, y'know, it was a good idea . . . and this commonwealth is a load of rubbish.

Q: And the title, could you explain what that means?

DEREK: "The sun never sweats on the British Empire," it's an old phrase.

Q: I thought it was "The sun never *sets* on the British Empire."

DEREK: Oh. I dunno. I dunno.

I'd heard it the other way. But basically the idea was . . . you had a phrase over here: "Don't Tread on Me." It's the same thing: The sun doesn't sweat on the empire. Y'know, it stays dry. It stays dry all the time, I thought was the idea. Like you wear your dress white and you go out in the afternoon. Somehow, the Brit stays dry; the woggies are mired in their own sweat of their own subjugation, but the Brit stays dry.

Q: Sort of like "Don't rain on my parade"?

DEREK: Well, you can rain on my parade, but it won't get me

wet! It was quasi-mystical in that sense. There was something about the idea of Britain as a place, as a source of ultimate dryness. I feel personally that that album is going to be our enduring contribution, because it takes the statement we make about power, dominance, and applies it to a people. It happens to be the British people, but so what? I think ultimately everybody can identify with that, even the woggies themselves. They'll just say, "Yeah, well, I *should* be dominated by them, that's a good idea, thank you."

Q: Moving along, when the triple-live LP *Jap Habit* was released in England, it broke fresh ground in terms of gimmick packaging—which has subsequently become something of a commonplace over there. But when it came out in the States, it naturally didn't have any of

those goodies—in fact, it had been reduced to just a *double*-live set. What were some of the packaging innovations that we may have missed?

DEREK: Let's see, there was a paper kimono, which Jeanine designed; and there was some do-it-yourself origami, including an origami replica of the devil's head; and I think we put some raw fish in there, like sushi? Little pieces of raw tuna with some seaweed. It was an attention-getter, I'll say that. You knew that album was around: "Oh, you've got *Jap Habit*, do you?" "Yeah, how do you know?" "Oh, somethin' tells me." Like that.